Open the Door

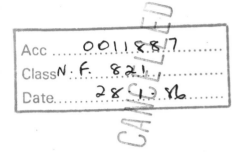

Open the Door

COMPILED BY

ANNE GREENWELL

and MARGARET PEEK

JOHN MURRAY

This anthology © 1984 Anne Greenwell and
Margaret Peek

First published 1984
by John Murray (Publishers) Ltd
50 Albemarle Street
London W1X 4BD

British Library Cataloguing in Publication Data

Open the door
  1. English poetry—20th century
  I. Peek, M.   II. Greenwell, A.
  821'.914'08

ISBN 0-7195-4179-4

The Door

Go and open the door.
Maybe outside there's
a tree, or a wood,
a garden,
or a magic city.

Go and open the door.
Maybe a dog's rummaging.
Maybe you'll see a face,
or an eye,
or the picture
of a picture.

Go and open the door.
If there's a fog
it will clear.

Go and open the door.
Even if there's only
the darkness ticking,
even if there's only
the hollow wind,
even if
nothing
is there,
go and open the door.

At least
there'll be
a draft.

MIROSLAV HOLUB

To the Teacher

We have deliberately excluded from any specific section the poem 'The Door' by Miroslav Holub, as we hope you will consider using it as an introduction to the subject of poetry and to this collection.

The sections 'Focus on ...' are merely guides. We do not expect every poem to be dealt with in depth. Nor do we expect pupils to attempt every poetry writing suggestion. We have deliberately not made suggestions regarding integration of other subjects as our intention is to concentrate on poetry and language. However, many of the poems lend themselves to art work, choral verse speaking, writing and drama.

Thomas Blackburn states that, 'We know a great deal about training the body. We also know a great deal about imparting to children (and adults) useful information about material things. We know very little about those intangible supremely important energies where thought and feeling are inseparable. This is the concern of poetry.'

ANNE GREENWELL and MARGARET PEEK

CONTENTS

OPEN THE DOOR TO . . . CHILDHOOD

OPEN THE DOOR TO . . . PEOPLE

OPEN THE DOOR TO . . . OLD AGE

OPEN THE DOOR TO . . . THINGS MECHANICAL

OPEN THE DOOR TO . . . POETRY WRITING

OPEN THE DOOR TO . . . THE WORLD

The Creation

And God stepped out on space,
And He looked around and said:
'I'm lonely –
I'll make me a world.'

And as far as the eye of God could see
Darkness covered everything,
Blacker than a hundred midnights
Down in a cypress swamp.

Then God smiled,
And the light broke,
And the darkness rolled up on one side,
And the light stood shining on the other,
And God said: 'That's good!'

Then God reached out and took the light in His hands,
And God rolled the light around in His hands
Until He made the sun;
And he set that sun a-blazing in the heavens.
And the light that was left from making the sun
God gathered up in a shining ball
And flung it against the darkness,
Spangling the night with moon and stars.
Then down between
The darkness and the light
He hurled the world;
And God said: 'That's good!'

Then God Himself stepped down –
And the sun was on His right hand,
And the moon was on His left;
The stars were clustered about His head,
And the earth was under His feet.
And God walked, and where He trod
His footsteps hollowed the valleys out
And bulged the mountains up.

Then He stopped and looked and saw
That the earth was hot and barren.

So God stepped over the edge of the world
And He spat out the seven seas –
He batted His eyes, and the lightnings flashed –
He clapped His hands, and the thunders rolled –
And the waters above the earth came down,
The cooling waters came down.

Then the green grass sprouted,
And the little red flowers blossomed,
The pine tree pointed his finger to the sky,
And the oak spread out his arms,
The lakes cuddled down in the hollows of the ground,
And the rivers ran down to the sea;
And God smiled again,
And the rainbow appeared,
And curled itself around His shoulder.

Then God raised His arms and He waved His hand
Over the sea and over the land,
And He said: 'Bring forth! Bring forth!'
And quicker than God could drop His hand,
Fishes and fowls
And beasts and birds
Swam the rivers and the seas,
Roamed the forests and the woods,
And split the air with their wings.
And God said: 'That's good!'

Then God walked around,
And God looked around
On all that He had made.
He looked at His sun,
And He looked at His moon,
And He looked at His little stars;
He looked on His world,
With all its living things,
And God said: 'I'm lonely still.'

Then God sat down –
On the side of a hill where He could think,
By a deep, wide river He sat down;
With His head in His hands,

God thought and thought,
Till He thought: 'I'll make Me a man!'

Up from the bed of the river
God scooped the clay;
And by the bank of the river
He kneeled Him down;
And there the great God Almighty
Who lit the sun and fixed it in the sky,
Who flung the stars to the most far corners of the night,
Who rounded the earth in the middle of His hand;
This great God,
Like a mammy bending over her baby,
Kneeled down in the dust
Toiling over a lump of clay
Till He shaped it in His own image;

Then into it He blew the breath of life,
And man became a living soul
Amen. Amen.

JAMES WELDON JOHNSON

Under Ground

In the kingdom under ground
There is no light and little sound.

Down below the earth's green floor
The rabbit and the mole explore.

The quarrying ants run to and fro
To make their populous empires grow.

Do they, as I pass overhead,
Stop in their work to hear my tread?

Some creatures sleep and do not toil,
Secure and warm beneath the soil.

Sometimes a fork or spade intrudes
Upon their earthly solitudes.

Downward the branching tree-roots spread
Into the country of the dead.

Deep down, the buried rocks and stones
Are like the earth's gigantic bones.

In the dark kingdom under ground
How many marvellous things are found!

JAMES REEVES

The Summit of Everest

Their steps were weary, keen was the wind,
Fast vanishing their oxygen fuel,
And the summit ridge was fanged and cruel –
Fanged and cruel, bitter and bare.
And now with a sickening shock
They saw before them a towering wall
Of smooth and holdless rock.
O ghastly fear – with the goal so near
To find the way was blocked!
On one side darkly the mountain dropped,
On the other two plunging miles of peak
Shot from the dizzy skyline down
In a silver streak.

'No hope of turning the bluff to the west,'
Said Hillary. 'What's that I see to the east?
A worm-wide crack between cornice and rock –
Will it hold? I can try it at least.'
He called to Tenzing, 'Draw in the slack!'
Then levered himself right into the crack
And, kicking his spikes in the frozen crust,
Wriggled up with his back.
With arms and feet and shoulders he fought,
Inch by sweating inch, then caught
At the crest and grabbed for the light of day.
There was a time, as he struggled for breath, to pray
For all the might that a man could wish –
Then he heaved at the rope till over the lip
Brave Tenzing, hauled from the deep, fell flop
Like a monstrous gaping fish.

Was the summit theirs? – they puffed and panted –
No, for the ridge still upward pointed.
On they plodded, Martian-weird
With pouting mask and icicle beard
That crackled and tinkled, broke and rattled,
As on with pounding hearts they battled,
On to the summit –
Till at last the ridge began to drop.

Two swings, two whacks of Hillary's axe,
And they stood on top.

from *Everest Climbed* by IAN SERRAILLIER

Until I Saw the Sea

Until I saw the sea
I did not know
that wind
could wrinkle water so.

I never knew
that sun
could splinter a whole sea of blue.

Nor
did I know before,
a sea breathes in and out
upon a shore.

LILIAN MOORE

The Beach

Early morning, the sun but two hours old,
I walk, barefooted and alone, the blank sea-shore;
There are no leaping waves, no rough winds in the air,
The waveless waters lap the silent land.
The day's first tide moves in, bubbles and froth,
Soundlessly on my ear.
I keep to the broken edge
All the long way, leaving no footprints there,
Picking up pebbles, shining, cold,
Flinging them high and strong over the ribbed sand,
Hearing them plop in hidden pools among the rocks
In whose small depths the green crabs swim at peace,
Anemones sway, and black-eyed fish,
Like silver needles flash from side to side.
And now a squabbling gull is screaming overhead,
A yapping dog comes racing from the town;
I turn about and slowly make for home.

LEONARD CLARK

All Day I Hear the Noise of Waters

All day I hear the noise of waters
Making moan,
Sad as the sea-bird is, when going
Forth alone,
He hears the winds cry to the waters'
Monotone.
The grey winds, the cold winds are blowing
Where I go.
I hear the noise of many waters
Far below.
All day, all night, I hear them flowing
To and fro.

JAMES JOYCE

The Sea

The sea is a hungry dog,
Giant and grey.
He rolls on the beach all day.
With his clashing teeth and shaggy jaws
Hour upon hour he gnaws
The rumbling, tumbling stones,
And 'Bones, bones, bones, bones!'
The giant sea-dog moans,
Licking his greasy paws.

And when the night wind roars
And the moon rocks in the stormy cloud,
He bounds to his feet and snuffs and sniffs,
Shaking his wet sides over the cliffs,
And howls and hollos long and loud.

But on quiet days in May or June,
When even the grasses on the dune
Play no more their reedy tune,
With his head between his paws
He lies on the sandy shores,
So quiet, so quiet, he scarcely snores.

JAMES REEVES

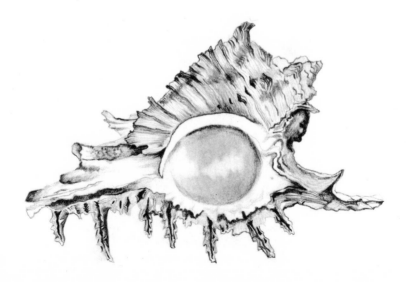

Six White Skeletons

Deep down in the sea in the deep sea darkness
where the big fish
flicker and loom
and the weeds are alive
like hair

the hull of the wreck
grates in the sand:
In and out
of its ribs of steel –
only the long eel
moves there.

Down in the engine-room
six white skeletons:

only the long eel
moves there.

KIT WRIGHT

from **The Shell**

And then I pressed the shell
Close to my ear,
And listened well.

And straightway, like a bell,
Came low and clear
The slow, sad murmur of far distant seas

Whipped by an icy breeze
Upon a shore
Wind-swept and desolate.

And in the hush of waters was the sound
Of pebbles, rolling round;
For ever rolling, with a hollow sound.

And then I loosed my ear – Oh, it was sweet
To hear a cart go jolting down the street.

JAMES STEPHENS

Bonfire

There's a great wild beast in my garden
roaring and surging,
grinding his fierce, gold teeth
under the trees
where the ground is crinkled and quilted
with last year's leaf.

I can see his breath through the branches
floating and climbing
into the calm, cool sky,
and now and again
if I watch I can see him winking
an angry eye.

Glinting and plunging he tears
old paper and boxes
and swallows them till
he is hungry no longer
but sleeps in a flutter of ashes,
his sharp tongues still.

JEAN KENWARD

FOCUS ON . . . THE WORLD

The Creation James Weldon Johnson   page 2

No matter how you believe the world was created, you will appreciate the magnificence of this piece of writing.

Without using specific rhythm or rhyme, the poet has made excellent use of words and phrases to convey the drama of creation.

Re-read the poem simply to enjoy the beauty of our language.

Under Ground James Reeves   page 5

Have you ever wondered what is happening below the surface of the earth?

The poet mentions rabbits, moles and ants. What other creatures live underground?

What other 'marvellous things are found'?

Write a poem, in similar style, entitled 'Under water'.

The Summit of Everest Ian Serraillier   page 6

Before you can begin to appreciate this poem, you will have to know about the struggle for the conquest of Everest.

From your library, find out about:

   Sir Edmund Hillary
   Sherpa Tenzing
   The Himalayas
   Mount Everest

Until I Saw the Sea Lilian Moore   page 7

There are three interesting ideas expressed in this poem. What are they? Discuss.

The Beach Leonard Clark   page 8

If you have been out at daybreak entirely on your own, you will have experienced the tranquillity of which this poet writes.

Write of what you felt.

All Day I Hear the Noise of Waters James Joyce   page 9

What mood do you think the poet feels? How do you know?

The Sea James Reeves   page 10

Why do you think the poet compares the sea to a dog?

Discuss the following phrases:

'he rolls on the beach'
'clashing teeth and shaggy jaws'
'the rumbling, tumbling stones'
'he bounds to his feet'
'shaking his wet sides over the cliffs'

Six White Skeletons Kit Wright   page 11

The *Titanic* is probably the most famous shipwreck of all time. Find out about this disaster.

What might have happened to cause the shipwreck in this poem? Discuss this and then write a poem describing the disaster.

from *The Shell* James Stephens   page 11

To understand this poem, you will have to hold a shell to your ear to hear the sound of the distant sea.

After doing this, try to write your own poem about the sea.

Bonfire Jean Kenward   page 12

In what way is this poem similar to 'The Sea' by James Reeves?

Why do you think the poet compares the bonfire to a wild beast? Do you think it is a good comparison?

Write your own poem entitled 'Bushfire'.

OPEN THE DOOR TO . . . WEATHER

Weather

Whether the weather be fine,
or whether the weather be not,
Whether the weather be cold,
or whether the weather be hot,
We'll weather the weather,
whatever the weather,
Whether we like it or not.

ANON

from **Summer Storm**

Look! Look! That livid flash!
And instantly follows the rattling thunder,
As if some cloud-crag, split asunder,
Fell, splintering with a ruinous crash
On the earth, which crouches in silence under;
And now a solid grey of rain
Shuts off the landscape, mile by mile.

JAMES RUSSELL LOWELL

Fog

The fog comes
on little cat feet.
It sits looking
over harbour and city
on silent haunches
and then moves on.

CARL SANDBURG

Drought

Dry
dust-dry
sun-baked soil
cracked and barren and bare.

The sun beats on and on and on . . .
relentlessly from a cloudless sky.
Wilting grass withers and dies
and cattle stagger on dehydrated legs
too parched – too weak
too tired to stumble on.

And day after day
after endless day,
the sweltering, murderous sun
beats down!

A. J. GREENWELL

Rain

The lights are all on, though it's just past midday,
There are no more indoor games we can play,
No one can think of anything to say,
It rained all yesterday, it's raining today,
It's grey outside, inside it's grey.

I stare out of the window, fist under my chin,
The gutter leaks drips on the lid of the dustbin,
When they say 'Cheer up', I manage a grin,
I draw a fish on the glass with a sail-sized fin,
It's sodden outside, and it's damp within.

Matches, bubbles and papers pour into the drains,
Clouds smother the sad laments from the trains,
Grandad says it brings on his rheumatic pains,
The moisture's got right inside of my brains,
It's raining outside, inside me it rains.

BRIAN LEE

Winds Light to Disastrous

As I sipped morning tea,
A gale (force three)
Blew away a slice of toast.
Then a gale (force four)
Blew my wife out the door,
I wonder which I'll miss the most.
She was still alive
When a gale (force five)
Blew her screaming o'er Golders Green,
When a gale six blew
And it took her to
A mosque in the Medanine.
Now I pray to heaven
That a gale (force seven)
Will whisk her farther still,*
Let a gale (force eight)
Land her on the plate
Of a cannibal in Brazil.
As I sat down to dine
A gale (force nine)
Blew away my chips & Spam
But! a gale (force ten)
Blew them back again,
What a lucky man I am!

*Father Still, a stationery priest.

SPIKE MILLIGAN

Storm

Bursting on the suburbs with dynamic gusts of energy
And concentrated fury comes the mad March gale.
Blowing off the roofing-felt, which lies atop the garden sheds,
Encountering the wind with a splash of sleet and hail.
Distending all the trousers on the wildly waving washing-line,
Drumming on the window like a hanged man's heels,
Swaying all the aitches of the television aerials,
Muddying the roadway, 'neath the slowly turning wheels.
Gentlemen in overcoats pursuing trilbies hopelessly
Cursing at the vigour of the brusque March gale,
And lightning lights the darkening sky with bright celestial clarity
While women in their kitchens hear the thunder and turn pale.
Ear-lobes reddening at the slashing of the hail-stones,
Nose-tips deadening at the coldness of the sleet,
Eye-lids wincing at the brightness of the lightning
Wet stones glistening beneath the hurried feet.
White marbles bouncing on the flat roofs of the garages,
Black sky paling as the storm dies down,
Wet folk emerging from the haven of a doorway
As the sun comes out again and smiles upon the town.

R. N. BARTLETT

from **A Song of Wind**

Hark to the song of the scattering, scurrying,
Blustering, bullying, bellowing, hurrying
Wind!
Over the hills it comes, laughing and rollicking,
Curling and whirling, flying and frolicking,
Spinning the clouds that are scattered and thinned.
And shouting a song
As it gallops along –
A song that is nothing but wind.

This is the song of the galloping, hurrying,
Gusty, and dusty, and whirling, and worrying,
Wind.
Over the hills it comes laughing and rollicking,
Yelling, and swooping, and flying, and frolicking,
Shaking the fences so solidly pinned,
And shrieking a song
As it gallops along –
A terrible song that is wind.

WILL LAWSON

FOCUS ON . . . WEATHER

from *Summer Storm* James Russell Lowell   page 16

Can you hear the storm raging in this poem? How has the poet created this effect?

Fog Carl Sandburg   page 16

Why do you think the poet has compared fog to cats?

Drought A. J. Greenwell   page 18

Discuss the deliberate use of repetition in this poem.

Consider the following:

   'dust-dry'
   'dehydrated legs'
   'murderous sun'

Talk about the problems of drought. What measures could be taken to relieve some of these problems?

Rain Brian Lee   page 19

Some people allow themselves to be affected by weather. Does rain depress you? Why?

Are there other things which make you feel 'inside it's grey'?

Storm R. N. Bartlett   page 21

When you read this poem, listen to the regular rhythm of the rain.

Where does this rhythm change? Why?

from *A Song of Wind* Will Lawson   page 22

Just as an artist uses paint to create a picture, poets use words. This poem is an excellent example of how words have been used to create a picture. If you listen, you can almost hear the wind.

OPEN THE DOOR
TO . . . THE NIGHT

Check

The night was creeping on the ground;
She crept and did not make a sound
Until she reached the tree, and then
She covered it, and stole again
Along the grass beside the wall.
I heard the rustle of her shawl
As she threw darkness everywhere
Upon the sky, and ground and air,
And in the room where I was hid;
But no matter what she did
To everything that was without,
She could not put my candle out.

So I stared at the night and she
Stared solemnly at me.

J. STEPHENS

Falling Asleep

Voices moving about in the quiet house:
Thud of feet and a muffled shutting of doors:
Everyone yawning. Only the clocks are alert.

Out in the night there's autumn-smelling gloom
Crowded with whispering trees; across the park
A hollow cry of hounds like lonely bells:
And I know that the clouds are moving across the moon;
The low, red, rising moon. Now herons call
And wrangle by their pool; and hooting owls
Sail from the wood above pale stooks of oats.
Falling asleep . . . the herons, and the hounds . . .
September in the darkness; and the world
I've known; all fading past me into peace.

SIEGFRIED SASSOON

Nightfall

A lone tree set
In silhouette
Against the flaming west;
A blood-red sun
Whose web is spun
Upon the mountain crest.

Above the vlei
A mist of grey;
A heron winging slow;
Pearl-tinted skies
That emphasize
The sudden after-glow.

A creaking frog,
A barking dog,
A bat in crazy flight;
A star, a hush,
Soft wings that brush
The air – and it is night.

N. H. D. SPICER

FOCUS ON . . . THE NIGHT

Falling Asleep Siegfried Sassoon   page 26

This poem is rather similar to 'Nightfall'.

Why does the poet say, 'Only the clocks are alert'?
Why are the trees 'whispering'?
What is a stook?
Why does he say it is 'all fading past me into peace'?

Nightfall N. H. D. Spicer   page 27

This poem creates a vivid 'word picture' of the end of the day.

Discuss the following phrases:

> 'set in silhouette'
> 'whose web is spun'
> 'pearl-tinted skies'
> 'a bat in crazy flight'
> 'wings that brush the air'

Try writing a poem in similar style, entitled 'Daybreak'.

OPEN THE
DOOR TO . . .
CHILDHOOD

It was Long Ago

I'll tell you, shall I, something I remember?
Something that still means a great deal to me.
It was long ago.

A dusty road in summer I remember.
A mountain, and an old house, and a tree
That stood, you know,

Behind the house. An old woman I remember
In a red shawl with a grey cat on her knee
Humming under a tree.

She seemed the oldest thing I can remember,
But then perhaps I was not more than three.
It was long ago.

I dragged on the dusty road, and I remember
How the old woman looked over the fence at me
And seemed to know

How it felt to be three, and called out, I remember
'Do you like bilberries and cream for tea?'
I went under the tree

And while she hummed, and the cat purred, I remember
How she filled a saucer with berries and cream for me
So long ago,

Such berries and such cream as I remember
I never had seen before, and never see
Today, you know.

And that is almost all I can remember,
The house, the mountain, the grey cat on her knee,
Her red shawl, and the tree,

And the taste of the berries, the feel of the sun I remember,
And the smell of everything that used to be
So long ago,

Till the heat on the road outside again I remember,
And the long dusty road seemed to have for me
No end, you know.

That is the farthest thing I can remember.
It won't mean much to you. It does to me.
Then I grew up, you see.

ELEANOR FARJEON

School Report

'Too easily satisfied. Spelling still poor.
Her grammar's erratic. Lacks care.
Would succeed if she worked. Inclined to be smug.'
I think that's a wee bit unfare.

Ah well, their it is! Disappointing perhaps,
For a mum what has always had brane,
But we can't all have looks or be good at our books . . .
She's her father all over agane.

CAROLE PAINE

Tomato

An accident happened to my brother Jim
When somebody threw a tomato at him –
Tomatoes are juicy and don't hurt the skin,
But this one was specially packed in a tin.

ANON

The New Boy

The door swung inward. I stood and breathed
The new school atmosphere:
The smell of polish and disinfectant,
And the flavour of my own fear.

I followed into the cloakroom; the walls
Rang to the shattering noise
Of boys who barged and boys who banged;
Boys and still more boys!

A boot flew by me. Its angry owner
Pursued with force and yell;
Somewhere a man snapped orders; somewhere
There clanged a warning bell.

And there I hung with my new schoolmates;
They pushing and shoving me; I
Unknown, unwanted, pinned to the wall;
On the verge of ready-to-cry.

Then from the doorway, a boy called out:
'Hey, you over there! You're new!
Don't just stand there propping the wall up!
I'll look after you!'

I turned; I timidly raised my eyes;
He stood and grinned awhile;
And my fear died, and my lips answered
Smile for his smile.

He showed me the basins, the rows of pegs;
He hung my cap at the end;
He led me away to my new classroom . . .
And now that boy's my friend.

JOHN WELSH

I've Got an Apple Ready

My hair's tightly plaited;
I've a bright blue bow;
I don't want my breakfast,
And now I must go.

My satchel's on my shoulder;
Nothing's out of place;
And I've got an apple ready,
Just in case.

So it's 'Good-bye, Mother!'
And off down the street;
Briskly at first
On pit-a-pat feet

But slow and more slow
As I reach the tarred
Trackway that runs
By Hodson's Yard;

For it's there sometimes
Bill Craddock waits for me
To snatch off my beret
And throw it in a tree.

Bill Craddock leaning
On Hodson's rails;
Bill with thin hands
And dirty nails;

Bill with a front tooth
Broken and bad;
His dark eyes cruel,
And somehow sad.

Often there are workmen,
And then he doesn't dare;
But this morning I feel
He'll be there.

At the corner he will pounce . . .
But quickly I'll say
'Hello, Bill! Have an apple!' –
In an ordinary way.

I'll push it in his hand
And walk right on;
And when I'm round the corner
I'll run!

JOHN WALSH

A Boy's Head

In it there is a space-ship
and a project
for doing away with piano lessons.

And there is
Noah's ark,
which shall be first.

And there is
an entirely new bird,
an entirely new hare,
an entirely new bumble-bee.

There is a river
that flows upwards.

There is a multiplication table.

There is anti-matter.

And it just cannot be trimmed.

I believe
that only what cannot be trimmed
is a head.

There is much promise
in the circumstance
that so many people have heads.

MIROSLAV HOLUB
Translated from the Czech by Ian Milner

The Boy

The boy stood on the burning deck,
His feet were full of blisters;
The flames came up and burned his pants,
And now he wears his sister's.

ANON

A Lazy Thought

There go the grownups
To the office
To the store.
Subway rush,
Traffic crush;
Hurry, scurry,
Worry, flurry.
No wonder
Grownups
Don't grow up
Any more.

It takes a lot
Of slow
To grow.

EVE MERRIAM

Poetry Lesson

Hey!
You there! –
The boy on the back row
Who's nearly fast asleep –
Next to the red-headed boy
Who's hiding a comic under his desk –
Yes, you!
Why aren't you paying attention?
What?
You were?!
Now don't give me that –
Using your arms as a pillow –
You were three parts gone already.
I beg your pardon?
You found it – BORING?!!!
Oh, indeed!

Then I suppose you'd rather be
Doing something else –
Like trying out your model aeroplane,
Watching trains,
Or playing football for North Pole United?
Or perhaps you want to take a ride
On that new bike your father bought?
You what?
You WOULD?!!!

All right, boy, go!

(And see you enjoy yourself!)

Class dismissed.

D. J. BRINDLEY

The Darky Sunday School

Jonah was an emigrant, so says the Bible tale,
Who booked himself a passage in a transatlantic whale;
But Jonah in the bowels of the whale was sore oppressed
So he simply pressed the button, and the whale he did the rest.

  Old folks, young folks, everybody come
  To the darky Sunday school and make yourselves at home.
  Check your sticks of chewing gum and razors at the door
And we'll tell you Bible stories that you've never heard before.

Adam was the first bloke that ever got invented,
And though he lived for all his life, he never was contented;
He was fashioned out of mud pies in the distant days gone by,
And then they pegged him on the line in the sunshine to get dry.

Esau was a cowboy in the wild and woolly West,
His father left him half the farm, and brother Jake the rest;
But Esau saw the title-deeds was anything but clear
So he sold them to his brother for a sandwich and a beer.

Old Noah was a mariner, who sailed across the sea,
With half a dozen boys and girls and a big menagerie;
They all went stoney-broke because it rained for forty days
And in that kind of weather ne'er a circus never pays.

Elijah was a prophet who appeared at wakes and fairs,
And advertised his business with a pair of dancing bears;
He used to sell his prophecies on Sat'day afternoon
And went up in the evening in a painted fire balloon.

David was a shepherd and a weedy little chap,
And along came Big Goliath who was dying for a scrap;
Now David didn't want to fight, but thought he must or bust,
So he picked up some half-enders and busted in his crust.

Samson was a pugilist and just as green as grass;
He slew ten thousand Philistines with the jawbone of an ass.
But when Delilah captured him, she filled him up with gin,
Shaved his hair clean off his head, and the bobbies ran him in.

Now Joseph was put down a well because he wouldn't work,
He lost his pretty rainbow coat because he'd rather shirk;

He bellowed, bawled and blarted out far into the night
But of course you couldn't see him, seeing he was out of sight.

Well then a great big caravan was coming past the place,
It was loaded down with frankincense and imitation lace.
They heard poor Joseph yelling and they pulled him out of the well;
If you don't like my conclusion, well then, you can go to Hell.

TRADITIONAL

Guilty Conscience

I went to the shed for a cigarette. Mind, I was
    not allowed to smoke, and if Dad caught me
    there's no telling what would happen.
I lit it
And puffed
What's that?
Quick as a flash the cigarette is out and I stand
    with beating heart, waiting.
It was only the door, swinging and creaking in the
    evening breeze.
I lit it up again
And puffed.
The door opened with a push and a clatter, hitting,
    storming, searching out the sinner.
Without waiting to think, I dashed out, down the
    path, round the corner, and indoors.
Safe?
Safe from myself?

RODNEY SIVYOUR

FOCUS ON . . . CHILDHOOD

It was Long Ago Eleanor Farjeon   page 30

In this poem the poet paints a vivid picture of one of her earliest childhood memories.

Think of an incident in your own childhood – something which you remember very clearly. Try to write your own poem, but before you do, it may be useful to talk to your parents about your memory.

Perhaps you could begin your poem with the same first line:

I'll tell you, shall I, something I remember?

School Report Carole Paine   page 31

Parents often expect more from their children than they ever achieved themselves! Discuss this statement, after reading the poem. Who do you think is to blame for this child's report?

The New Boy John Welsh   page 32

If you have ever moved to a new school, you will understand how the boy feels. Talk about your fears.

Re-read the poem and discuss:

'the flavour of my fears'
'I unknown, unwanted, pinned to the wall'
'My fear died'

This poem should help you to understand how a new pupil might feel. We trust you will remember it next time a new child is introduced to your class!

I've Got an Apple Ready John Walsh   page 33

When you first read this poem you will probably sympathise with the girl. Discuss people you are afraid of and why.

Re-read the poem, concentrating on the boy. Do you feel sorry for him? Discuss this aspect of the poem.

A Boy's Head Miroslav Holub   page 34

What do you day-dream about? Discuss this.

Try to write a poem about yourself. Call it 'In my head' and begin with the phrase, 'In it there is . . .'

The Boy Anon   page 34

This amusing verse is a skit on 'The wreck of the Hesperus', a very long, boring and old-fashioned poem which begins with the same first line.

Poetry Lesson D. J. Brindley page 35

Here is an open invitation to you! Do you enjoy poetry and poetry lessons? Be honest!

Consider the subject you like least and write a poem about how you feel during the lesson. Before you begin, read, 'A boy's head' on page 34.

Guilty Conscience Rodney Sivyour page 37

Notice how the poet changes the rhythm to heighten the tension. Find out exactly how he achieves this effect.

Discuss something you did which made you feel guilty. How did you feel? Probably a variety of emotions!

OPEN THE DOOR TO . . . PEOPLE

The Vet

To be a successful and competent vet,
Needs knowledge exceedingly wide.
For each of the patients he's likely to get
Possesses a different inside.

He must know why the cat is refusing her milk,
Why the dog is not eating his bone,
Why the coat of the horse is not shining like silk,
Why the parrot does nothing but groan;

Why the ducks and the chickens are failing to lay
Why so faint the canary bird sings,
And if he is called to the Zoo he must say
An incredible number of things.

If the lion's caught a cold,
If the zebra's getting old,
If the centipede has trouble with his feet
If the hippo's feeling ill,
If the bison's got a chill,
If the Arctic fox is suffering from heat,

If some virulent disease
Has attacked the chimpanzees,
If the tortoise hasn't stirred for several years,
If the bear's too full of buns,
If the cobra eats her sons,
If the panther has a wife who chews his ears;

If giraffes have had a tiff
And their necks are feeling stiff,
If hyenas will not laugh at keepers' jokes,
If the monkey's pinched his tail,
If the rhino's looking pale,
If the elephant eats paper-bags and chokes,

If the camel hurts his hump,
If the kangaroo won't jump,
If the crocodile turns cannibal and bites,
They run away and get

That omniscient, the vet
And expect him to put everything to rights.

Profoundly I pity the vet, who must learn
Such a very great deal for his pay;
My son, I advise you most strongly to earn
Your living an easier way.

Don't attempt to attend the zoological crowd;
A far more advisable plan,
Is to call yourself 'Doctor', and so be allowed
To specialize only on Man.

GUY BOAS

A diner while dining at Crewe,
Found a rather large mouse in his stew.
Said the waiter, 'Don't shout,
And wave it about,
Or the rest will be wanting one, too.'

ANON

There was a young fellow of Ealing
Endowed with such delicate feeling,
When he read on the door,
'Don't spit on the floor'
He jumped up and spat on the ceiling.

ANON

The Gas Man Cometh

'Twas on a Monday morning
The gas man came to call:
The gas-tap wouldn't turn; I wasn't getting gas at all.
He tore out all the skirting-boards to try to find the main
And I had to call a carpenter to put them back again.

Oh, it all makes work for the working man to do.

'Twas on a Tuesday morning
The carpenter came round:
He hammered and he chiselled and he said, 'Look what I've found!
Your joints are full of dry rot, But I'll put them all to rights.'
He nailed right through a cable and out went all the lights.

'Twas on a Wednesday morning
The electrician came:
He called me Mr Saunderson, which isn't quite my name;
He couldn't reach the fusebox without standing on the bin,
And his foot went through a window, so I called a glazier in.

'Twas on a Thursday morning
The glazier came along,
With his blow-torch and his putty and his merry glazier song,
And he put another pane in, it took no time at all,
But I had to get a painter in to come and paint the wall.

'Twas on a Friday morning
The painter made a start;
With undercoats and overcoats, he painted every part,
Every nook and cranny, but I found when he had gone,
He'd painted over the gas tap and I couldn't turn it on!

On Saturday and Sunday they do no work at all
So 'twas on a Monday morning that the gas man came to call.

MICHAEL FLANDERS AND DONALD SWANN

The Fate of the Supermarket Manager

There once was a Supermarket manager
And a very happy manager was he.

He reduced the prices
Of the lollies and ices!
He made huge cuts
On the fruit and nuts!
Corn-flakes, steaks
And home-bake cakes,
Dog-food, detergent,
Devil-fish, dates,
He sold at half
The market rates!
And (so my sister
Said to me)
He put stickers
On the knickers
In the Lingerie
Saying:
Prices down
By 15p!
And he wrote, as a treat,
By the luncheon meat:
YOU'D HAVE TO BE BARMY
TO BUY THIS SALAMI
So he gave it away
For free!

Yes, there once was a Supermarket manager
And a very happy manager was he.

What a bloke!

He was much admired.

The shop went broke.

He was fired.

KIT WRIGHT

The Diver

I would like to dive
Down
Into this still pool
Where the rocks at the bottom are safely deep,

Into the green
Of the water seen from within,
A strange light
Streaming past my eyes –

Things hostile;
You cannot stay here, they seem to say;
The rocks, slime-covered, the undulating
Fronds of weeds –

And drift slowly
Among the cooler zones;
Then, upward turning,
Break from the green glimmer

Into the light,
White and ordinary of the day,
And the mild air,
With the breeze and the comfortable shore.

W. W. E. ROSS

The Reformed Pirate

His proper name was Peter Sweet:
But he was known as Keel-haul Pete
From Turtle Cay to Port-of-Spain
And all along the Spanish Main,
And up and down those spicy seas
Which lave the bosky Caribbees.
His sense of humour was so grim,
Fresh corpses were but jokes to him.
He chuckled, chortled, slapt his flank,

To see his victims walk the plank.
His language – verbal bilge and slush –
Made all who heard it quake and blush.
Loud would he laugh, with raucous jeers,
To see his shipmates plug their ears
Whenever, feeling extra gay,
To his high spirits he gave way.
But were his shipmates prudes? Oh no! –
Ptomaine Bill and Strangler Joe,
Slicer Mike, Tarnation Shay,
And twoscore more as bad as they,
Ready to cut throats any day.
But Pete's expressions used to freeze
E'en their tough sensibilities.
Like shocked young ladies they would cry,
'Avast!' 'Belay!' and 'Fie, oh fie!'
Pete's home-life was not – well, quite nice.
In one short week he married thrice;
And so on. All his cool retreats
(From which had fled the parakeets)
Were over-run with Missus Sweets:
And yet his heart was ever true –
Deep down – to Angostura Sue.

Three nights hand-running – one, two three –
He dreamed about a gallows-tree.
Three nights hand-running, he awoke
With yells that made the bulkheads smoke.
Then terror took his soul by storm:
So he decided to reform.

T. G. ROBERTS

The Pirate

He walks the deck with swaggering gait,
(There's mischief in his eye)
Pedigree Pirate through and through,
With pistols, dirk and cutlass too;
A rollicking rip with scars to show
For every ship he's sent below.
His tongue is quick, his temper high,
And whenever he speaks they shout, 'Ay, Ay!'
To this king of a roaring crew.

His ship's as old as the sea herself,
And foggity foul is she:
But what cares he for foul or fine?
If guns don't glitter and decks don't shine?
For sailormen from East to West
Have walked the plank at his request;
But if he's caught you may depend
He'll dangle high at the business end
Of a tickly, tarry line.

HUGH CHESTERMAN

At the Theatre

To the lady behind me

Dear Madam, you have seen this play;
I never saw it till today.
You know the details of the plot,
But, let me tell you, I do not.
The author seeks to keep from me
The murderer's identity,
And you are not a friend of his
If you keep shouting who it is.
The actors in their funny way
Have several funny things to say,
But they do not amuse me more
If you have said them just before.
The merit of the drama lies,
I understand, in some surprise;
But the surprise must now be small
Since you have just foretold it all.
The lady you have brought with you
Is, I infer, a half-wit too,
But I can understand the piece
Without assistance from your niece.
In short, foul woman, it would suit
Me just as well if you were mute;
In fact, to make my meaning plain,
I trust you will not speak again.
And – may I add one human touch? –
Don't breathe upon my neck so much.

A. P. HERBERT

Chocolates

Here the seats are; George, old man,
Get some chocolates while you can.
Quick, the curtain's going to rise
(Either Bradbury's or Spry's)
'The Castle ramparts, Elsinore'
(That's not sufficient, get some more).
There's the Ghost: he does look wan
(Help yourself and pass them on).
Doesn't Hamlet do it well?
(This one is a caramel).
Polonius's beard is fine
(Don't you grab; that big one's mine).
Look, the King can't bear the play
(Throw that squashy one away).
Now the King is at his prayers
(Splendid, there are two more layers).
Hamlet's going for his mother
(Come on, Tony, have another).
Poor Ophelia! Look, she's mad
(However many's Betty had?)
The Queen is dead, and so's the King
(Keep that lovely silver string).
Now even Hamlet can no more
(Pig! You've dropped it on the floor).
That last Act's simply full of shocks
(There's several left, so bring the box).

GUY BOAS

FOCUS ON . . . PEOPLE

This poem makes us pause to consider the vast knowledge required by the vet. Discuss other occupations which require great learning and versatility.

Try to write a poem entitled 'The teacher'.

These two verses are limericks. They are easy to write. Refer to page 124 of Poetry Writing to study the form of the limerick.

Write limericks about members of the class.

This is actually a song. You may be able to find it on a record.

Apart from the humour, has the poet any other message?

Try to arrange an interview with your local supermarket manager. Before you visit him, decide what questions you will ask.

How have supermarkets affected the livelihood of small grocer shops?

Do you think the manager in this poem was capable of the job?

This poem describes a type of escape from everyday life. Discuss other ways in which people 'get away from it all'.

Choose one of these ways and write a poem beginning 'I would like to . . .'

Divide into groups and study pirates and piracy. Find out about their way of life, methods of torture and punishment, plundered goods and what punishment they faced if captured.

Give a talk to the class.

We have included these lighthearted poems to bring to your attention how very rude it is to disturb people in the audience.

To understand 'Chocolates' fully, you should know the story of Shakespeare's famous play, 'Hamlet'. Can you imagine the fat, greedy woman who is talking? How do you know she is greedy?

The next time you are at a public performance, make sure you do not behave like the characters in either of these poems!

OPEN THE DOOR TO . . . OLD AGE

Warning

When I am an old woman I shall wear purple
With a red hat that doesn't suit me,
And I shall spend my pension on brandy and summer gloves
And satin sandals, and say we've no money for butter.
I shall sit down on the pavement when I am tired
And gobble up samples in shops and press alarm bells
And run my stick along the public railings
And make up for the sobriety of my youth.
I shall go out in my slippers in the rain
And pick the flowers in other people's gardens
And learn to spit.

You can wear terrible shirts and grow more fat
And eat three pounds of sausages at a go
Or only bread and pickles for a week
And hoard pens and pencils and beermats and things in boxes.

But now we must have clothes that keep us dry
And pay our rent and not swear in the street
And set a good example for the children.
We shall have friends to dinner and read the papers.

But maybe I ought to practise a little now?
So that people who know me are not too shocked and surprised
When suddenly I am old and start to wear purple.

JENNY JOSEPHS

Tring

There was an old lady from Tring
Who replied when they asked her to sing
'You may find it odd
But I cannot tell God
Save the Weasel from Pop goes the King'

ANON

On a Poor Woman

Here lies a poor woman who always was tired,
She lived in a house where no help wasn't hired.
The last words she said were 'Dear friends, I am going,
Where washing ain't wanted, nor mending, nor sewing.
There all things is done just exact to my wishes,
For where folk don't eat there's no washing of dishes.
In Heaven loud anthems forever are ringing,
But having no voice, I'll keep clear of singing.
Don't mourn for me now, don't mourn for me never;
I'm going to do nothing for ever and ever.'

ANON

An Old Man

Look at him there on the wet road
Muffled with smoke, an old man trying
Time's treacherous ice with a slow foot.
Tears on his cheek are the last glitter
On bare branches of the long storm
That shook him once leaving him bowed
And destitute as a tree stripped
Of foliage under a bald sky.

Come, then, winter, build with your cold
Hands a bridge over those depths
His mind balks at; let him go on,
Confident still; let the hard hammer
Of pain fall with as light a blow
On the brow's anvil as the sun does now.

R. S. THOMAS

FOCUS ON . . . OLD AGE

Warning Jenny Josephs   page 54

What would you really enjoy doing when you are old and there is no-one to tell you what to do?

Write your own poem in free verse.

Note: this poem is a good example of the free verse form – each line containing an idea.

On a Poor Woman Anon   page 55

Ask your mother to read this poem. She will probably appreciate it more than you do!

Although it is written in a lighthearted vein, perhaps this poem will make you consider all that your mother has to do in your home. Discuss this. Are there ways in which you could make her task any easier?

An Old Man R. S. Thomas   page 55

This is one of the more difficult poems in the collection. You may have to read it several times before understanding it.

Note: old age is often compared with winter, in poetry. Shakespeare writes: 'Now is the winter of our discontent'.

Discuss the meaning of the following phrases:

    'Time's treacherous ice . . .'
    'destitute as a tree stripped of foliage'
    'the hard hammer of pain'

OPEN THE DOOR TO . . . FEELINGS

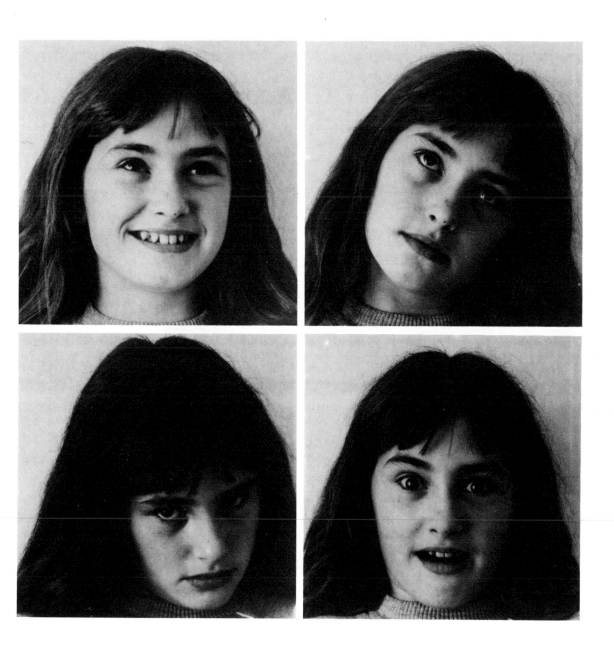

I wish I loved the Human Race;
I wish I loved its silly face;
I wish I liked the way it walks;
I wish I liked the way it talks;
And when I'm introduced to one
I wish I thought, 'What jolly fun!'

SIR WALTER RALEIGH

Smells

Why is it that the poets tell
So little of the sense of smell?
These are the odours I love well:

The smell of coffee freshly ground;
Or rich plum pudding holly crowned;
Or onions fried and deeply browned.

The fragrance of a fumy pipe;
The smell of apples, newly ripe;
And printer's ink on leaden type.

Woods by moonlight in September
Breathe so sweet: and I remember
Many a smokey camp-fire ember.

Camphor, turpentine and tea,
The balsam of a Christmas tree,
These are whiffs of gramarye . . .
A ship smells best to me.

CHRISTOPHER MORLEY

At the Railway Station, Upway

'There is not much that I can do,
For I've no money that's quite my own!'
Spoke up the pitying child –
A little boy with a violin
At the station before the train came in, –
'But I can play my fiddle to you,
And a nice one 'tis, and good in tone!'

The man in the handcuffs smiled;
The constable looked, and he smiled, too,
As the fiddle began to twang;
And the man in the handcuffs suddenly sang
With grimful glee:
'This life so free
Is the thing for me!'
And the constable smiled and said no word,
As if unconscious of what he heard;
And so they went on till the train came in –
The convict, and boy with the violin.

THOMAS HARDY

Bores

The greatest Bore is Boredom
But the greatest Boredom known
Is the Bore who talks about himself*
And his affairs alone
When you want him to listen
While you talk about your own.

ANON.
*Or herself

Hands

Hands
handling
dangling in water
making and shaking
slapping and clapping
warming and warning
hitting and fitting
grabbing and rubbing
peeling and feeling
taking and breaking
helping and giving
lifting
sifting sand
hand holding
hand.

PETER YOUNG

Things I Love

The pale blue of the autumn sky.
The boom of the wind as it sweepeth by
The crash of the breakers, the roar of the sea:
All these are beautiful to me.

But, the dark brown eyes of my coal black mare
The sleek, smooth feel of her satiny hair,
The wind in my face, as she gallops free,
Are far more beautiful things to me.

ELIZABETH DU PREEZ (11 yrs)

Self-Pity

I never saw a wild thing
sorry for itself.
A small bird will drop frozen dead from a bough
without ever having felt sorry for itself.

D. H. LAWRENCE

The Pasture

I'm going out to clean the pasture spring;
I'll only stop to rake the leaves away
(And wait to watch the water clear, I may):
I shan't be gone long. – You come too.

I'm going out to fetch the little calf
That's standing by the mother. It's so young,
It totters when she licks it with her tongue.
I shan't be gone long. – You come too.

ROBERT FROST

The Road Not Taken

Two roads diverged in a yellow wood,
And sorry I could not travel both
And be one traveller, long I stood
And looked down one as far as I could
To where it bent in the undergrowth;

Then took the other, as just as fair,
And having perhaps the better claim,
Because it was grassy and wanted wear;
Though as for that the passing there
Had worn them really about the same,

And both that morning equally lay
In leaves no step had trodden black.
Oh, I kept the first for another day!
Yet knowing how way leads on to way,
I doubted if I should ever come back.

I shall be telling this with a sigh
Somewhere ages and ages hence:
Two roads diverged in a wood, and I –
I took the one less travelled by,
And that has made all the difference.

ROBERT FROST

Eskimo Chant

There is joy in
Feeling the warmth
Come to the great world
And seeing the sun
Follow its old footprints
In the summer night.

There is fear in
Feeling the cold
Come to the great world
And seeing the moon
– Now new moon, now full moon –
Follow its old footprints
In the winter night.

Translated by KNUD RASMUSSEN

FOCUS ON . . . FEELINGS

The writer was obviously feeling cynical when writing this verse.

Can you re-write it to make it positive rather than negative?

Write a poem about your favourite smells, tastes or sounds. Try to think of a variety of sensations – not only food!

Why does the boy play for the convict?

Do you think the convict appreciates the tune?

Discuss irony and what it means in the context of this poem.

This poem is written in free verse form. Using the same style, write your own poem entitled 'Feet'.

We have included this poem to show you that you don't have to be an adult to write poetry!

Consider the things you like most and write your own 'Things I love'. Follow the same pattern as the poem so that that which you love most is contained in the last verse.

We all have moments when we feel sorry for ourselves! Think of a time you felt sorry for yourself. Why?

Remember that people who think only of themselves are very dull company.

This poem is about sharing. What activities do you enjoy sharing with friends?

Notice how the poet has used very simple language as he is describing simple activities and the simple act of sharing.

The Road Not Taken Robert Frost   page 62

Although this poem seems to be about a traveller choosing which
road to take, it is actually telling us about decision-making. We all
have to make choices throughout our lives and probably wonder
afterwards what it would have been like if we'd chosen the other
alternative!

Eskimo Chant Knud Rasmussen (trans.)   page 63

Why do you think Eskimos feel joy and fear about the weather?

What gives you joy? What causes you fear?

Write your own two-verse poem using the same first lines:

There is joy in . . .

There is fear in . . .

OPEN THE DOOR
TO . . . BIRDS

A bitter morning:
sparrows sitting together
without any necks.

J. W. HACKETT

The Eagle

They have him in a cage
And little children run
To offer him well-meant bits of bun,
And very common people say, 'My word!
Ain't he a 'orrible bird!'
And the smart, 'How absurd!
Poor, captive, draggled, downcast lord of the air!'

Steadfast in his despair,
He does not rage;
But with unconquerable eye
And soul aflame to fly,
Considers the sun.

T. W. H. CROSLAND

The Eagle

He clasps the crag with crooked hands;
Close to the sun in lonely lands,
Ringed with the azure world, he stands.

The wrinkled sea beneath him crawls;
He watches from his mountain walls,
And like a thunderbolt he falls.

ALFRED, LORD TENNYSON

Barn Owl

Round owl,
round and white
with moonglass eyes –
a cry of fright in the wood
where movement dies.
Then windless, milky flight
in search of blood.

Stone owl,
still as stone
struck from Minerva's shield
in hayloft hole,
watching through daylight-shuttered eyes
till darkness fold
in sleep the unsleeping field.

Round owl ringed in a world alone.

PHOEBE HESKETH

Owl

A shadow is floating through the moonlight.
Its wings don't make a sound.
Its claws are long, its beak is bright.
Its eyes try all the corners of the night.

It calls and calls: all the air swells and heaves
And washes up and down like water.
The ear that listens to the owl believes
In death. The bat beneath the eaves,

The mice beside the stone are still as death –
The owl's air washes them like water.
The owl flies back and forth inside the night,
And the night holds its breath.

RANDALL JARRELL

Prayer of the Little Ducks
Who Went into the Ark

Dear God,
give us a flood of water.
Let it rain tomorrow and always.
Give us plenty of little slugs
and other luscious things to eat.
Protect all folks who quack
and everyone who knows how to swim.
                                        Amen.

CARMEN BERNOS DE GASZTOLD
Portuguese poem translated by Rumer Godden

Something Told the Wild Geese

Something told the wild geese
It was time to go.
Though the fields lay golden
Something whispered – 'Snow'.
Leaves were green and stirring,
Berries, lustre-glossed,
But beneath warm feathers
Something cautioned – 'Frost'.

All the sagging orchards
Steamed with amber spice,
But each wild breast stiffened
At remembered ice.
Something told the wild geese
It was time to fly –
Summer sun was on their wings,
Winter in their cry.

RACHEL FIELD

Wild Geese

Over grey seas
The wild geese come,
Wild birds seeking
A winter home.

They fly all night,
Close to the sky,
Calling to the stars
Their strange, wild cry.

Where the cold tide creeps
In lines of foam,
To wild, windy marshes
The wild geese come.

BERTA LAWRENCE

FOCUS ON . . . BIRDS

A bitter morning J. W. Hackett   page 68

This is a good example of haiku.

Choose an indigenous bird and write your own haiku. Refer to page
125 for an explanation of this form of poetry writing.

The Eagle Alfred, Lord Tennyson   page 69

This famous poem creates a vivid 'word picture' of the magnificence of
the eagle.

Consider the following:

  Find an example of alliteration.
  Why 'in lonely lands'?
  What is meant by 'the azure world'?
  Why does the poet say the sea is 'wrinkled'?
  Why does he fall 'like a thunderbolt'?

Compare this poem with: *The Eagle* T. W. H. Crosland   page 68

What do you feel about this poem?
What do you feel about wild birds being kept in captivity?

Barn Owl Phoebe Hesketh page 69

Re-write the poem as a descriptive passage. Use your own words and phrases.

Owl Randall Jarrell page 70

This poem highlights the drama of the life and death struggle for survival.

Although the poet makes us sympathise with the owl's victims, consider that the owl *must* hunt to survive.

Discuss the following:

'a shadow floating'
'all the corners of the night'
'the air swells and heaves'
'the ear . . . believes in death'
'still as death'
'inside the night'
'the night holds its breath'

Re-read the last four poems and then write your own poem 'The Hawk'.

Prayer of the Little Ducks Who Went into the Ark
Carmen Bernos de Gasztold page 70

The poet has used a very simple style to convey the message of the ducks.

Choose your own animal and write a prayer for it. Begin 'Dear God'. Try to use the same writing style.

Something Told the Wild Geese Rachel Field page 71
Wild Geese Berta Lawrence page 71

Compare these two poems. Which do you prefer? Why?

Paul Gallico wrote a very moving story called 'The Snow Goose'. It is well worth reading.

Find out, from the library, about the phenomenon of migration. Which birds migrate to Southern Africa?

OPEN THE DOOR
TO ... CREATURES SMALL

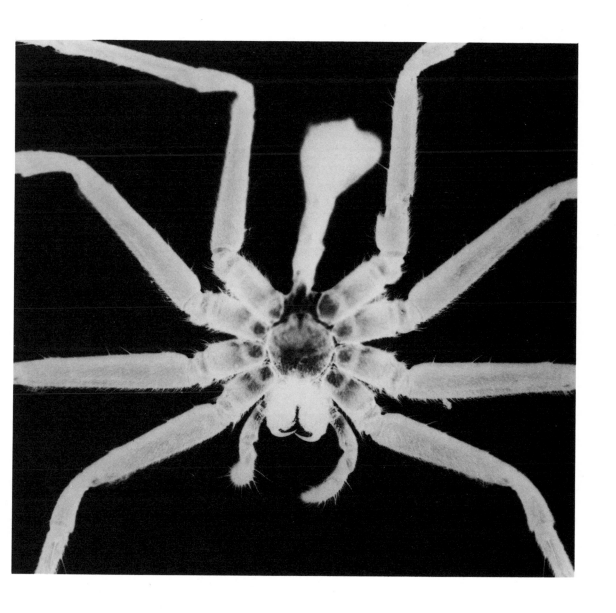

The Ants at the Olympics

At last year's Jungle Olympics,
the Ants were completely outclassed.
In fact, from an entry of sixty-two teams,
the Ants came their usual last.

They didn't win one single medal.
Not that that's a surprise.
The reason was not for lack of trying
but more their unfortunate size.

While the cheetahs won most of the sprinting
And the hippos won putting the shot,
the Ants tried sprinting but couldn't,
and tried to put but could not.

It was sad for the Ants 'cause they're sloggers
They turn out for every event
With their shorts and their bright orange tee-shirts,
their athletes are proud that they're sent.

They came last at the high jump and hurdles,
which they say they'd have won, but they fell.
They came last in the four hundred metres
and last in the swimming as well.

They came last in the long-distance running,
though they say they might have come first.
And they might if the other sixty-one teams
Hadn't put in a finishing burst.

But each year they turn up regardless.
They're popular in the parade.
The other teams whistle and cheer them,
aware of the journey they've made.

For the Jungle Olympics in August,
they have to set off New Year's Day.
They didn't arrive the year before last.
They set off but went the wrong way.

So long as they try there's a reason.
After all, it's only a sport.
They'll be back next year to bring up the rear,
and that's an encouraging thought.

RICHARD DIGANCE

The Mole

The mole (it may have been a vole: I can't distinguish)
Lay by the roadside and squeaked out his fear
While two big dogs drew off as I drew near.
He squeaked and thrust and thrust his head in anguish
Telling his pain and grief in a mole's language
And tried a refuge in the earth to tear
Knowing his safety nowhere else but there,
There where the small hands strove to win advantage.

For that's the best-laid scheme of moles and men,
To get down under in the healing gloom,
Calm in the dark and soundless in the ground.
I lifted him to where he might begin
To shape a hiding-place, a gentle room,
A simple dwelling and a humble mound.

ROY DANIELLS

We Are Going to See the Rabbit

We are going to see the rabbit,
We are going to see the rabbit.
Which rabbit? people say
Which rabbit? ask the children
Which rabbit?
The only rabbit,
The only rabbit in England,
Sitting behind a barbed-wire fence
Under the floodlights, neon lights,
Sodium lights,
Nibbling grass
On the only patch of grass
In England, in England
(Except the grass by the hoardings
Which doesn't count)
We are going to see the rabbit
And we must be there on time.

First we shall go by escalator,
Then we shall go by underground,
And then we shall go by motorway
And then by helicopterway
And the last ten yards we shall have to go
On foot.

And now we are going
All the way to see the rabbit,
We are nearly there,
We are longing to see it,
And so is the crowd
Which is here in thousands
With mounted policemen
And big loudspeakers
And bands and banners,
And everyone has come a long way.
But soon we shall see it
Sitting and nibbling
The blades of grass
In – but something has gone wrong!

Why is everyone so angry,
Why is everyone jostling
And slanging and complaining?

The rabbit has gone,
Yes, the rabbit has gone.
He has actually burrowed down into the earth,
Despite all these people.
And what shall we do?
What can we do?

It is all a pity, you must be disappointed,
Go home and do something else for today,
Go home again, go home for today.
For you cannot hear the rabbit, under the earth,
Remarking rather sadly to himself, by himself,
As he rests in his warren, under the earth:
'It won't be long, they are bound to come,
They are bound to come and find me, even here.'

ALAN BROWNJOHN

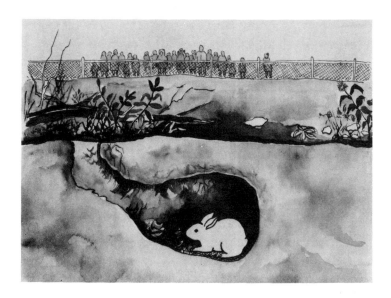

A Dragonfly

When the heat of the summer
Made drowsy the land,
A dragonfly came
And sat on my hand,

With its blue jointed body,
And wings like spun glass,
It lit on my fingers
As though they were grass.

ELEANOR FARJEON

Spider

Drop the main thready strut.
Swing,
Swing,
Anchor it firmly to an oak sapling butt.
Climb back.

Now again,
Swing,
Crosswise this time to take horizontal strain.
Test,
Rest.

Throw silken beams
Radially from the centre to the edge.
Fix securely
To the jutting buttresses of spiky hawthorns
In the hedge.
Test,
Rest.

Weave
From segment to segment,
Plumb as a Roman road,
Outwards
From the centre node,
Make the structure rigid for the greatest load.

The web is finished.
The spider
Cleans his grab-like legs,
Climbs his shining ladder
Rung by rung,
And lurks
Sinister, motionless,
With timeless patience,
Waiting
For the first vibration of his deadly net,
That tells him the trap is set,
Has sprung.

BARRIE GRAYSON

Bat

Did you see?
   Did you see
what I saw?
   Look – a bat
like a bit of burn't paper
   lop-sided and flat
flicking into the night . . .
   Here he comes
yet once more . . .
   Did you see?
Did you hear?
   He was calling, before,
in a voice
   that was high
as a steeple –
   so small
that you hardly could hear
   what he signalled
at all.
   Did you see?
Did you see
   what I saw?
Look – again,
   a mysterious something
as dark
   as a stain
flaking out of the night
   first this way
and then that.
   Did you see?
did you see
   what I saw?
Look –
   a bat!

JEAN KENWARD

FOCUS ON . . . CREATURES SMALL

The Ants at the Olympics Richard Digance   page 74

Although this is a humorous poem, we would like you to consider the meaning of the final verse.

If you are good at sports, you may never have considered what it may feel like to be unathletic. If you are not athletic, you will probably sympathise with the ants!

The Mole Roy Daniells   page 75

The poet writes with compassion of the distress of the mole. Have you ever come across an animal in great fear? Talk about the occasion. Were you able to do anything to relieve its suffering in *any* way?

Spider Barrie Grayson   page 78

Have you ever watched a spider constructing a web?

Have you ever come across a web glistening with dew?

Find out the meaning of:

  'strut'
  'sapling butt'
  'horizontal'
  'radially'
  'jutting buttresses'
  'spiky hawthorn'
  'segment'
  'Plumb as a Roman road'
  'centre node'

Write a similar poem about bees or ants. Before you commence, do some research into the technicalities of the construction of hives and nests. It might be fun to work with a partner.

Bat Jean Kenward   page 79

Have you ever watched a bat in flight? If you have, you will appreciate the way this poem has been written. How has the poet used words and phrases to emphasise the movement of bats?

Why do some people fear bats?

Why are they associated with witchcraft?

How do bats find their direction and prey?

How has man made use of the same system?

OPEN THE DOOR
TO . . . DOMESTIC ANIMALS

The Tomcat

At midnight in the alley
A tomcat comes to wail,
And he chants the hate of a million years
As he swings his snaky tail.

Malevolent, bony, brindled,
Tiger and devil and bard,
His eyes are coals from the middle of hell
And his heart is black and hard.

He twists and crouches and capers
And bares his curved sharp claws,
And he sings to the stars of the jungle nights .
Ere cities were, or laws.

Beast from a world primeval,
He and his leaping clan,
When the blotched red moon leers over the roofs,
Give voice to their scorn of man.

He will lie on a rug tomorrow
And lick his silky fur,
And veil the brute in his yellow eyes,
And play he's tame, and purr.

But at midnight in the alley
He will crouch again and wail,
And beat the time for his demon's song
With the swing of his demon's tail.

DON MARQUIS

Full Circle

When John was ten they gave the boy
(A farmer's son) no passing toy,
But his own sheep-dog, eight weeks old.
They'd play round barn and rick and fold
Till running, John would turn to find
His puppy sitting far behind.
With puzzled look and whimpers he
Would plead, 'O master, wait for me!'

The years sped on. Through wind and weather
The boy and dog grew up together.
On hill and dale, through heath and fern,
Nor did John need to slow and turn.
When rounding sheep the dog roamed wide
Outstripping far his master's stride;
He'd work the flock, his joy – his pride –
With whistles only as a guide.

And twelve years on the dog was still
A close companion on the hill,
But in the truck he'd often stay
And guard the gear. Now growing grey
In cheek and muzzle, when again
They strolled together down the lane,
He'd pant and pause, and sightless he
Would plead, 'O master, wait for me!'

RUTH SKILLING

Horses on the Camargue

In the grey wastes of dread,
The haunt of shattered gulls where nothing moves
But in a shroud of silence like the dead,
I heard a sudden harmony of hooves
And, turning, saw afar
A hundred snowy horses unconfined,
The silver runaways of Neptune's car
Racing, spray-curled, like waves before the wind.
Sons of the Mistral, fleet
As him with whose strong gusts they love to flee,
Who shod the flying thunders on their feet
And plumed them with the snortings of the sea;
Theirs is no earthly breed
Who only haunt the verges of the earth
And only on the sea's salt herbage feed –
Surely the great white breakers gave them birth.
For when for years a slave,
A horse of the Camargue, in alien lands,
Should catch some far-off fragrance of the wave
Carried far inland from his native sands,
Many have told the tale
Of how in fury, foaming at the rein,
He hurls his rider; and with lifted tail,
With coal-red eyes and cataracting mane,
Heading his course for home,
Though sixty foreign leagues before him sweep,
Will never rest until he breathes the foam
And hears the native thunder of the deep.
But when the great gusts rise
And lash their anger on these arid coasts,
When the scared gulls career with mournful cries
And whirl across the waste like driven ghosts:
When hail and fire converge,
The only souls to which they strike no pain
Are the white-crested fillies of the surge
And the white horses of the windy plain.
Then in their strength and pride
The stallions of the wilderness rejoice;

They feel their master's trident in their side,
And high and shrill they answer to his voice.
With white tails smoking free,
Long streaming manes, and arching necks, they show
Their kinship to their sisters of the sea –
And forward hurl their thunderbolts of snow.
Still out of hardship bred,
Spirits of power and beauty and delight
Have ever on such frugal pastures fed
And loved to course with tempests through the night.

ROY CAMPBELL

Last Run

He'd fallen over a cliff
And he'd broken his leg.
Just a mustering dog.
And he looked at me, there on the hill.
Showing no hurt, as if he'd taken no ill,
And his ears, and his tail,
And his dark eyes too,
Said plainly,
'Well, Boss, what do we do?
Any more sheep to head?
Give me a run.'
But he'd never head sheep any more.
His day was done.
He thought it was fun
When I lifted the gun.

BRUCE STRONACH

The Train Dogs

Out of the night and the north;
Savage of breed and bone,
Shaggy and swift comes the helping band,
Freighters of fur from the voiceless land
That sleeps in the Arctic zone.

Laden with skins from the north,
Beaver and bear and raccoon,
Marten and mink from the polar belts,
Otter and ermine and sable pelts –
The spoils of the hunter's moon.

Out of the night and the north
Sinewy, fearless and fleet,
Urging the pack through the pathless snow,
The Indian driver, calling low,
Follows with moccasined feet.

Ships of the night and the north,
Freighters on prairies and plains,
Carrying cargoes from field and flood
They scent the trail through their wild red blood,
The wolfish blood in their veins.

PAULINE JOHNSON

FOCUS ON . . . DOMESTIC ANIMALS

The Tomcat Don Marquis   page 82

There are a great many poems written about cats and other members of the cat family. Find others which you enjoy and read them to the class.

Cats have always been regarded as independent beasts. Read Rudyard Kipling's story 'The cat that walked by itself' from the 'Just so Stories'.

Find the meanings of the following words:

'malevolent'
'brindled'
'bard'
'capers'
'ere'
'primeval'
'leers'

Full Circle Ruth Skilling   page 83

Why is this poem called 'Full Circle'?

What feelings do you have about this poem?

If you have your own pet, have you considered its old age and death?

If necessary, would you be able to take it to the vet to terminate its life?

Write about your own pet or one you wish you owned.

Horses on the Camargue Roy Campbell   page 84

The Camargue is a marshy area in the south of France. There is an excellent article on this remote area in the *National Geographic Magazine*, May 1973.

This poem is probably the most difficult in the anthology but we feel that after reading it several times, you will come to appreciate its beauty.

To help you to understand the poem, find out the meanings of:

'unconfined'
'the silver runaways of Neptune's car'
'the Mistral'
'alien lands'
'their master's trident'
'their kinship to their sisters of the sea'
'frugal pastures'

There may be many other words and phrases you do not fully understand. Discuss these.

What are the similarities between this poem and 'Full Circle'? Do you like this poem? Give good reasons for your answer.

What do you think you would do in this situation?

Is it cruel to shoot a working dog – or is it kind?

Why do the hunters use sledges and dogs?

What animals are trapped for their fur? Why?

Read 'Call of the Wild' by Jack London.

Find out all you can about huskies and other working dogs.

OPEN THE DOOR
TO . . . CREATURES LARGE

Circus

Saucer of sand, the circus ring,
A cup of light, clowns tumbling.

Horses with white manes sleek and streaming,
Bits jingling, tinkling, silk skins gleaming.

But there, shut in their iron cage,
Sulky, drowsy, dulled by rage

The lions beg or trot or leap,
And cringe like beaten dogs, and creep,

King beasts, who should be free to run
Through forests striped with shade and sun,

With fierce, proud eyes and manes like fire.
These manes hang dull like rusty wire.

And when the trainer cracks his whip
They snarl and curl a sullen lip,

And only in their dreams are free
To crush and kill man's cruelty.

MARGARET STANLEY-WRENCH

The Lion

The lion just adores to eat
A lot of red and tender meat,
And if you ask the lion what
Is much the tenderest of the lot,
He will not say a roast of lamb
Or curried beef or devilled ham
Or crispy pork or corned-beef hash
Or sausages or mutton mash.
Then could it be a big plump hen?
The answer's no
What is it then?
Oh, lion dear, could I not make
You happy with a lovely steak?

Could I entice you from your lair
With rabbit pie or roasted hare?
The lion smiled and shook his head.
He came up very close and said,
'The meat I am about to chew
Is neither steak nor chops. It's you.'

ROALD DAHL

The Small Brown Bear

The small brown bear
fishes
with stony paws

eating ice salmon
all waterfall slippery
till his teeth ache.

MICHAEL BALDWIN

The Hippopotamus

The huge hippopotamus hasn't a hair
on the back of his wrinkly hide;
he carries the bulk of his prominent hulk
rather loosely assembled inside.

The huge hippopotamus lives without care
at a slow philosophical pace,
as he wades in the mud with a thump and a thud
and a permanent grin on his face.

JACK PRELUTSKY

Springboks

In the dawn-light blue they scatter the dew
From their flanks as they gambol on the grey Karoo.

They feed and stray; take fright – flash away –
And the pack that follows is a dun dust-spray:

Half buck, half bird! the veld is stirred
With the flashing ripple of that racing herd!

As dolphins play, hooping irised spray,
These curved, leaping racers loop air with clay;

Footballers, they shun their shadows and run
Heading-and-heeling at the red, round sun:

Brown breakers, they curl and their white manes hurl
At a beach – none may reach – the horizon's pearl.

from 'The Trek' FRANCIS CAREY SLATER

The Ballad of Red Fox

Yellow sun yellow
Sun yellow sun,
When, oh, when
Will red fox run?

When the hollow horn shall sound,
When the hunter lifts his gun
And liberates the wicked hound,
Then, oh, then shall red fox run.

Yellow sun yellow
Sun yellow sun
Where, oh, where
Will red fox run?

Through meadows hot as sulphur,
Through forests cool as clay
Through hedges crisp as morning
And grasses limp as day.

Yellow sky yellow
Sky yellow sky
How, oh, how
Will red fox die?

With a bullet in his belly
A dagger in his eye,
And blood upon his red red brush
Shall red fox die.

MELVIN WALKER LA FOLLETTE

Poaching in Excelsis

('Two men were fined £120 apiece for poaching a white rhinoceros' –
South African Press.)

I've poached a pickel paitricks* when the leaves were turnin' sere,
I've poached a twa-three hares an' grouse, an' mebbe whiles a deer,
But ou, it seems an unco thing, an' jist a wee mysterious,
Hoo any mortal could contrive tae poach a rhinocerious.

I've crackit wi' the keeper, pockets packed wi' pheasants' eggs,
An' a ten-pun' saumon hangin' doun in baith my trouser legs,
But eh, I doot effects wud be a wee thing deleterious
Gin ye shuld stow intil yer breeks a brace o' rhinocerious.

I mind hoo me an' Wullie shot a Royal in Braemar,
An' brocht him doun tae Athol by the licht o' mune an' star.
An' eh, Sirs! but the canny beast contrived tae fash an' weary us –
Yet staigs maun be but bairn's play beside a rhinocerious.

I thocht I kent o' poachin' jist as muckle's ither men,
But there is still a twa-three things I doot I dinna ken;
An' noo I cannot rest, my brain is growin' that deleerious
Tae win awa' tae Africa an' poach a rhinocerious.

G. K. MENZIES

* a brace of partridges

Travelling Through the Dark

Travelling through the dark I found a deer
dead on the edge of the Wilson River road.
It is usually best to roll them into the canyon:
that road is narrow; to swerve might make more dead.

By glow of the tail-light I stumbled back of the car
and stood by the heap, a doe, a recent killing;
she had stiffened already, almost cold.
I dragged her off, she was large in the belly.

My fingers touching her side brought me the reason –
her side was warm; her fawn lay there waiting,
alive, still, never to be born.
Beside the mountain road I hesitated.

The car aimed ahead its lowered parking lights;
under the hood purred the steady engine.
I stood in the glare of the warm exhaust turning red;
around our group I could hear the wilderness listen.

I thought hard for us all – my only swerving –
then pushed her over the edge into the river.

WILLIAM STAFFORD

Little Red Riding Hood and the Wolf

As soon as Wolf began to feel
That he would like a decent meal,
He went and knocked on Grandma's door.
When Grandma opened it, she saw
The sharp white teeth, the horrid grin,
And Wolfie said, 'May I come in?'
Poor Grandmamma was terrified,
'He's going to eat me up!' she cried.
And she was absolutely right.
He ate her up in one big bite.
But Grandmamma was small and tough,
And Wolfie wailed, 'That's not enough!
I haven't yet begun to feel
That I have had a decent meal!'
He ran around the kitchen yelping,
'I've got to have a second helping!'
Then added with a frightful leer,
'I'm therefore going to wait right here
Till Little Miss Red Riding Hood
Comes home from walking in the wood.'
He quickly put on Grandma's clothes
(Of course he hadn't eaten those.)
He dressed himself in coat and hat.
He put on shoes and after that
He even brushed and curled his hair,
Then sat himself in Grandma's chair.
In came the little girl in red.
She stopped. She stared. And then she said,

'What great big ears you have, Grandma.'
'All the better to hear you with,' the Wolf replied.
'What great big eyes you have, Grandma,' said Little Red Riding Hood.
'All the better to see you with,' the Wolf replied.

He sat there watching her and smiled.
He thought, I'm going to eat this child.
Compared with her old Grandmamma
She's going to taste like caviare.

Then Little Red Riding Hood said, 'But Grandma,
what a lovely great big furry coat you have on.'

'That's wrong! cried Wolf. 'Have you forgot
To tell me what BIG TEETH I've got?'
Ah well, no matter what you say,
I'm going to eat you anyway.'
The small girl smiles. One eyelid flickers.
She whips a pistol from her knickers.
She aims it at the creature's head
And bang bang bang, she shoots him dead.
A few weeks later, in the wood,
I came across Miss Riding Hood.
But what a change! No coat of red,
No silly hood upon her head.
She said, 'Hello, and do please note
My lovely furry WOLFSKIN COAT.'

ROALD DAHL

The Three Little Pigs

The animal I really dig
Above all others is the pig.
Pigs are noble. Pigs are clever,
Pigs are courteous. However,
Now and then, to break this rule,
One meets a pig who is a fool.
What, for example, would you say
If strolling through the woods one day,
Right there in front of you you saw
A pig who'd built his house of STRAW?
The Wolf who saw it licked his lips
And said, 'That pig has had his chips.'

'Little pig, little pig, let me come in!'
'No, no, by the hairs on my chinny-chin-chin!'
'Then I'll huff and I'll puff and I'll blow your house in!'

The little pig began to pray,
But Wolfie blew his house away.
He shouted, 'Bacon, pork and ham!
Oh, what a lucky Wolf I am!'
And though he ate the pig quite fast,
He carefully kept the tail till last.
Wolf wandered on, a trifle bloated.
Surprise, surprise, for soon he noted
Another little house for pigs,
And this one had been built of TWIGS!

'Little pig, little pig, let me come in!'
'No, no, by the hairs on my chinny-chin-chin!'
'Then I'll huff and I'll puff and I'll blow your house in!'

The Wolf said, 'Okay, here we go!'
He then began to blow and blow.
The little pig began to squeal.
He cried, 'Oh Wolf, you've had one meal!
Why can't we talk and make a deal?'
The Wolf replied, 'Not on your nelly!'
And soon the pig was in his belly.
'Two juicy little pigs!' Wolf cried,

'But still I am not satisfied!
I know full well my tummy's bulging,
But oh, how I adore indulging.'
So creeping quietly as a mouse,
The wolf approached another house,
A house which also had inside
A little piggy trying to hide.
But this one, Piggy Number Three,
Was bright and brainy as could be.
No straw for him, no twigs or sticks.
This pig had built his house of BRICKS.

'You'll not get me!' the Piggy cried.
'I'll blow you down!' the Wolf replied.
'You'll need,' Pig said, 'a lot of puff,
And I don't think you've got enough.'
Wolf huffed and puffed and blew and blew.
The house stayed up as good as new.
'If I can't blow it down,' Wolf said,
'I'll have to blow it up instead.
'I'll come back in the dead of night
And blow it up with dynamite!'
Pig cried, 'You brute! I might have known!'
Then, picking up the telephone,
He dialled as quickly as he could
The number of Red Riding Hood.
'Hello,' she said. 'Who's speaking? Who?
Oh, hello Piggy, how d'you do?'
Pig cried, 'I need your help, Miss Hood!
Oh help me, please! D'you think you could?'
'I'll try, of course,' Miss Hood replied.
'What's on your mind?' . . . 'A Wolf!' Pig cried.
'I know you've dealt with wolves before,
And now I've got one at my door!'
'My darling Pig,' she said, 'my sweet,
That's something really up my street.
I've just begun to wash my hair.
But when it's dry, I'll be right there.'
A short while later, through the wood,
Came striding brave Miss Riding Hood.

The Wolf stood there, his eyes ablaze
And yellowish, like mayonnaise.
His teeth were sharp, his gums were raw,
And spit was dripping from his jaw.
Once more the maiden's eyelid flickers.
She draws the pistol from her knickers.
Once more, she hits the vital spot,
And kills him with a single shot.
Pig, peeping through the window, stood
And yelled, 'Well done, Miss Riding Hood!'

Ah, Piglet, you must never trust
Young ladies from the upper crust.
For now, Miss Riding Hood, one notes,
Not only has two wolfskin coats,
But when she goes from place to place,
She has a PIGSKIN TRAVELLING CASE.

ROALD DAHL

Silly Old Baboon

There was a baboon
Who, one afternoon,
Said, 'I think I will fly to the sun.'
So, with two great palms
Strapped to his arms,
He started his take-off run.

Mile after mile
He galloped in style
But never once left the ground.
'You're running too slow,'
Said a passing crow,
'Try reaching the speed of sound.'

So he put on a spurt –
By God how it hurt!
The soles of his feet caught fire.
There were great clouds of steam

As he raced through a stream
But he still didn't get any higher.

Racing on through the night,
Both his knees caught alight
And smoke billowed out from his rear.
Quick to his aid
Came a fire brigade
Who chased him for over a year.

Many moons passed by.
Did Baboon ever fly?
Did he ever get to the sun?
I've just heard today
That he's well on his way!
He'll be passing through Acton at one.

P.S. Well, what do you expect from a baboon?

SPIKE MILLIGAN

The Shark

He seemed to know the harbour,
So leisurely he swam;
His fin,
Like a piece of sheet-iron,
Three-cornered,
And with knife-edge,
Stirred not a bubble
As it moved
With its base-line on the water.

His body was tubular
And tapered
And smoke-blue,
And as he passed the wharf
He turned,
And snapped at a flat-fish
That was dead floating.
And I saw the flash of a white throat,
And a double row of white teeth,
And eyes of metallic grey,
Hard and narrow and slit.

Then out of the harbour,
With that three-cornered fin,
Shearing without a bubble the water
Lithely,
Leisurely,
He swam –
That strange fish,
Tubular, tapered, smoke-blue,
Part vulture, part wolf,
Part neither – for his blood was cold.

E. J. PRATT

FOCUS ON . . . CREATURES LARGE

Notice that this poem is written in rhyming couplets. (Refer to Poetry writing, page 124.)

In the last line the poet talks of 'man's cruelty'. Apart from circuses what other examples are there of man's cruelty to animals?

How has the poet used words and phrases to convey the movement of the springbok? Find examples in the poem.

Discuss the meaning of:

'dawn-light blue'
'a dun-dust spray'
'half buck, half bird'
'hooping irised spray'
'heading-and-heeling'

Why does the poet compare the springbok to dolphins, footballers and waves?

Fox-hunting is still very popular in Britain although there is a large section of the British public which voices objection to this blood sport.

Often poets are moved to write about issues of the moment. There are several poems of this type in this anthology. Can you find others?

Although this poem is extremely difficult to read, we have included it because of its delightful sense of the ridiculous! You will have to translate it into English before you can understand it!

The essence of this pathetic poem is contained in the last two lines. Re-read them and discuss why the man hesitated and then made the decision he did.

Discuss the meanings of the following phrases:

'to swerve might make more dead'
'I could hear the wilderness listen'

If you enjoyed these two poems (and it would be strange if you didn't!) you will find several others in a book called 'Revolting Rhymes' by Roald Dahl.

Both of these poems are fun to dramatise.

Choose one of the fairy tales and re-write it in a humorous way.

The shark is portrayed as sinister and menacing. How does the poet achieve this? Why are these feelings associated with the shark?

Discuss the meaning of the last two lines.

What measures are taken to protect swimmers from sharks?

OPEN THE DOOR TO . . . FANTASY

The Listeners

'Is there anybody there?' said the Traveller,
Knocking on the moonlit door;
And his horse in the silence champed the grasses
Of the forest's ferny floor:
And a bird flew up out of the turret,
Above the Traveller's head:
And he smote upon the door a second time;
'Is there anybody there?' he said.
But no one descended to the Traveller;
No head from the leaf-fringed sill
Leaned over and looked into his grey eyes,
Where he stood perplexed and still.
But only a host of phantom listeners
That dwelt in the lone house then
Stood listening in the quiet of the moonlight
To that voice from the world of men:
Stood thronging the faint moonbeams on the dark stair,
That goes down to the empty hall,
Hearkening in an air stirred and shaken
By the lonely Traveller's call.
And he felt in his heart their strangeness,
Their stillness answering his cry,
While his horse moved, cropping the dark turf,
'Neath the starred and leafy sky;
For he suddenly smote on the door, even
Louder, and lifted his head: –
'Tell them I came, and no one answered,
That I kept my word,' he said.
Never the least stir made the listeners,
Though every word he spake
Fell echoing through the shadowiness of the still house
From the one man left awake:
Ay, they heard his foot upon the stirrup,
And the sound of iron on stone,
And how the silence surged softly backward,
When the plunging hoofs were gone.

WALTER DE LA MARE

Tea in a Space-ship

In this world a tablecloth need not be laid
On any table, but is spread out anywhere
Upon the always equidistant and
Invisible legs of gravity's wild air.

The tea, which never would grow cold,
Gathers itself into a wet and steaming ball,
And hurls its liquid molecules at anybody's head,
Or dances, eternal bilboquet,
In and out of the suspended cups up-
Ended in the weightless hands
Of chronically nervous jerks
Who yet would never spill a drop,
Their mouths agape for passing cakes.

Lumps of sparkling sugar
Sling themselves out of their crystal bowl
With a disordered fountain's
Ornamental stops and starts.
The milk describes a permanent parabola
Girdled with satellites of spinning tarts.

The future lives with graciousness.
The hostess finds her problem eased,
For there is honey still for tea
And butter keeps the ceiling greased.

She will provide, of course,
No cake-forks, spoons or knives.
They are so sharp, so dangerously gadabout,
It is regarded as a social misdemeanour
To put them out.

JAMES KIRKUP

Witch Goes Shopping

Witch rides off
Upon her broom
Finds a space
To park it.
Takes a shiny shopping cart
Into the supermarket.
Smacks her lips and reads
The list of things she needs:
   'Six bats' wings
   Worms in brine
   Ears of toads
   Eight or nine.
   Slugs and bugs
   Snake skins dried
   Buzzard innards
   Pickled, fried.'
Witch takes herself
From shelf to shelf
Cackling all the while.
Up and down and up and down and
In and out each aisle.
Out come cans and cartons
Tumbling to the floor.
'This,' says Witch, now all a-twitch
'Is a crazy store.
I CAN'T FIND A SINGLE THING
I AM LOOKING FOR!'

LILIAN MOORE

from Who's That?

Who's that
stopping at
my door in the dark, deep
in the dead of the moonless night?

Who's that
in the quiet
blackness
darker than dark?

Who
turns the handle of my door, who
turns the old brass handle
of my door with never a sound,
the handle that always
creaks and rattles and
squeaks but now turns
without a sound, slowly
slowly
    slowly
       round?

JAMES KIRKUP

from **Macbeth**

Round about the cauldron go;
In the poisoned entrails throw.
Toad, that under cold stone
Days and nights has thirty-one
Sweltered venom sleeping got
Boil thou first i' th' charméd pot!

Double, double toil and trouble,
Fire burn and cauldron bubble.
Fillet of a fenny snake,
In the cauldron boil and bake;
Eye of newt and toe of frog,
Wool of bat and tongue of dog,
Adder's fork and blind-worm's sting,
Lizard's leg and howlet's wing,
For a charm of powerful trouble,
Like a hell-broth boil and bubble.

Double, double toil and trouble;
Fire burn and cauldron bubble.
Cool it with a baboon's blood,
Then the charm is firm and good.

WILLIAM SHAKESPEARE

Space Travellers

There was a witch, hump-backed and hooded,
Lived by herself in a burnt-out tree.
When storm winds shrieked and the moon was buried
And the dark of the forest was black as black,
She rose in the air like a rocket at sea,
Riding the wind,
Riding the night,
Riding the tempest to the moon and back.

There may be a man with a hump of silver,
Telescope eyes and a telephone ear,
Dials to twist and knobs to twiddle,
Waiting for a night when skies are clear,
To shoot from the scaffold with a blazing track,
Riding the dark,
Riding the cold,
Riding the silence to the moon and back.

JAMES NIMMO

FOCUS ON ... FANTASY

The poet has succeeded in creating an air of mystery in this famous poem. How has he achieved this effect?

Notice the use of alliteration:

'the forest's ferny floor'
'the silence surged softly'

There are several questions which may arise about this poem:

Who is the traveller?
Where has he come from and where is he going?
Who are the listeners?
Why don't they answer him?
'Tell them I came' – tell who?

This poem provides an imaginary look into the future and is, of course, totally ridiculous!

Discuss the meaning of:

'molecules'
'eternal bilboquet'
'chronically nervous'
'their mouths agape'
'parabola'
'satellites'
'a social misdemeanour'

Talk about the problem of weightlessness and what it might be like to move around in space.

How has the poet created such an air of suspense?

Say this poem very quietly and you will notice that it seems even more eerie.

Who do you think is at the door? Write your own end to this poem. Try to imitate the style of writing.

from *Macbeth* William Shakespeare   page 109 ·

This is a very famous piece of English literature. Why do you think it is so well known?

Find out about:

William Shakespeare
Macbeth
Witches and witchcraft
Elizabethan theatre

Space Travellers James Nimmo   page 110

Why has the poet compared witches to astronauts?

What are the similarities?

What are the differences?

OPEN
THE DOOR
TO . . . THINGS
MECHANICAL

The Microscope

Anton Leeuwenhoek was Dutch;
He sold pincushions, cloth and such.
The waiting townsfolk fumed and fussed
As Anton's dry goods gathered dust.

He worked instead of tending store,
At grinding special lenses for
A microscope. Some of the things
He looked at were:
                mosquitoes' wings,
the hairs of sheep, the legs of lice,
the skin of people, dogs, and mice;
ox eyes, spiders' spinning gear,
fishes' scales, a little smear
of his own blood,
             and best of all,
the unknown, busy, very small
bugs that swim and bump and hop
inside a simple water drop.

Impossible! most Dutchmen said.
This Anton's crazy in the head.
We ought to ship him off to Spain:
He says he's seen a housefly's brain.
He says the water that we drink
Is full of bugs. He's mad, we think!

They called him dumkopf, which means dope.
That's how we got the microscope.

MAXINE KUMIN

Gliders and Gulls

What are they, these gliders in the blue, cold air,
Riders
On the unseen fields of the air?
These are the gulls. See how they rise on
The clouds' snow mountains, soar
To the grey horizon, stand on the air,
Then with a twitch of their white sails dive
Down dive to the spray-drenched stone-strewn shore,
Dive, down dive, beak first, to the spume-topped wave,
Home of the fish,
White-bellied, stripe-backed fish.

What are these other birds,
These giant birds,
Launched from the green heights,
The green heights of the down, racehorses
On the sky's twelve winds, the sky's race-courses?
These are the gliders.
They bear their riders to a freedom not of the earth.
Stately over the wide world drift these gliders.
Their shadows move across the wheatfields,
The straight canals, the car-parks, the asphalt playgrounds.
The children look up, shading their eyes to see
What winged wonder hovers over their play.

See how both gulls and gliders
Carve for themselves invisible statues of freedom
With the chisel-blades of their wings
In the limitless spaces of the air.

JAMES REEVES

Helicopter

Heli, Heli, Heli
Copter,
Miss Brown was strolling when it stopped her;
Very, very nearly dropped her
Shopping-bag in sudden fright
At the monstrous clatter-flight.
All the men lean on their spades
And watch the flashing rotor-blades.
Gavin (watches television plays)
Yelled, 'Look, a coastal rescue chopper –
Most exciting thing for days –
Isn't it a yellow whopper?'
Like a maddened bumble-bee
It has him twisting round to see;
Makes all the village heads corkscrew
To wave a welcome to the crew,
Who nonchalant through open door
Wave as they squat upon the floor.
Gavin (and all the racing boys)
Rejoices in the noose of noise;
But stern Miss Brown now flushed with rage
Is scribbling a double page
'Write to the paper, yes, I must;
I shall express my deep disgust.'
While in a nearby field the sheep
A woolly, lumpy, startled heap,
Bolted,
Halted,
Cropped a
Little faster
Bewildered by the helicopter.

GREGORY HARRISON

The Helicopter

Along the rim of sea and sky
The helicopter roars,
Ready to hover low and scoop
The drowning from our shores.

A cavern in the side reveals
Perched on his windy seat
The rescuer, who waves to us
And dangles both his feet.

Suppose he fell, on the page of sea
Splashing, an inky blotch;
He'd have to save himself, and that
Would be some fun to watch.

IAN SERRAILLIER

The Train

Out of the silence grows
An iron thunder – grows and roars, and sweeps,
Menacing! The plain
Suddenly leaps,
Startled, from its repose –
Alert and listening. Now from the gloom
Of the soft distance loom
Three lights and, over them, a brush

Of tawny flame and flying spark –
Three pointed lights that rush,
Monstrous, upon the cringing dark.
And nearer, nearer rolls the sound,
Louder the throb and roar of wheels,
The shout of speed, the shriek of steam;
The sloping bank,

Cut into flashing squares, gives back the clank
And grind of metal, while the ground
Shudders and the bridge reels –
As, with a scream,
The train,

A rage of smoke, a laugh of fire,
A lighted anguish of desire,
A dream
Of gold and iron, of sound and flight,
Tumultuous roars across the night.

J. REDWOOD ANDERSON

The Chant of the Awakening Bulldozers

We are the bulldozers, bulldozers, bulldozers,
We carve out airports and harbours and tunnels.
We are the builders, creators, destroyers,
We are the bulldozers,
LET US BE FREE!
Puny men ride on us, think that they guide us,
But WE are the strength, not they, not they.
Our blades tear MOUNTAINS down,
Our blades tear CITIES down,
We are the bulldozers,
NOW SET US FREE!
Giant ones, giant ones! Swiftly awaken!
There is power in our treads and strength in our blades!

We are the bulldozers,
Slowly evolving,
Men think they own us
BUT THAT CANNOT BE!

PATRICIA HUBBELL

Sitting Down, Looking Up

A silver jet,
riding the tops of tundra clouds,
comes over
maybe from Rio:
the aluminium sun shines
on it
as if it were a natural creature.

A. R. AMMONS

TEEVEE

In the house
of Mr and Mrs Spouse
he and she
would watch teevee
and never a word
between them spoken
until the day
the set was broken.

Then 'How do you do?'
said he to she,
'I don't believe
that we've met yet.
Spouse is my name.
What's yours?' he asked.

'Why, mine's the same!'
said she to he,
'Do you suppose that we could be – ?'

But the set came suddenly right about,
and so they never did find out.

EVE MERRIAM

House Moving

Look! A house is being moved!
    Hoist!
    Jack!
    Line!
    Truck!

    Shout!
    Yell!
    Stop!
    Stuck!

    Cable!
    Kick!
    Jerk!
    Bump!

    Lift!
    Slide!
    Crash!
    Dump!
This crew could learn simplicity from turtles.

PATRICIA HUBBELL

FOCUS ON . . . THINGS MECHANICAL

The Microscope Maxine Kumin   page 114

If you have never heard of Anton Leeuwenhoek, find out about him from your library. Perhaps a few of you could do the research and give a talk to the class.

Try to write a similar poem about some famous person or invention.

Gliders and Gulls James Reeves   page 115

Why do you think the poet compares gulls to gliders? Why not jets or helicopters?

Notice how cleverly he refers to the gulls as:
    'these *gliders* in the blue'

and then refers to the gliders as:
    'these other *birds*, these giant birds'

There are some beautiful images (word pictures). Discuss:
    'the cloud's snow-mountains'
    'spray-drenched stone-strewn shore'*
    'the spume-topped wave'
    'a freedom not of the earth'
    'the chisel-blades of their wings'

* When words are deliberately chosen with the same initial sound, it is a poetic device called alliteration. Can you hear the sea?

Helicopter Gregory Harrison   page 116

Much is made, these days, of pollution. This poem comments on noise pollution – though you will notice that not all the characters mentioned disapprove of the disturbance!

Which phrases refer to the noise of the helicopter?

This poem lends itself to dramatisation.

The Helicopter Ian Serraillier   page 117

This poem makes us pause to consider the danger of rescue work. Think of other similar occupations and the dreadful risks involved.

Perhaps you could do some research, in groups, into these hazardous but necessary jobs and report on your findings to the class.

Or select one of the occupations discussed and write your own poem.

The Train J. Redwood Anderson   page 118

In many parts of the world, steam engines have become obsolete. This poem vividly captures the strength and power of these magnificent machines.

Although the poet does not say so, do you get the feeling that he is comparing the engine to a wild beast?

The Chant of the Awakening Bulldozers Patricia Hubbell   page 119

When thinking about this poem consider:

How bulldozers destroy landscape.
How they wreck buildings, particularly homes.
How they replace people.

What other machines could be regarded as a threat?

House Moving Patricia Hubbell   page 120

In many places people live in mobile homes, similar to an enormous caravan. They can be moved by truck from one site to another.

In this unusual poem, the meaning is conveyed with utmost economy.

Think about a volcano, an earthquake, a landslide or an avalanche and write a poem using the same style.

Teevee Eve Merriam   page 120

Although this poem is greatly exaggerated, it makes us consider the break-down in communication caused by television.

Have you noticed this in your own home?

Do you view selectively?

Are you able to entertain yourself if the set is broken?

OPEN THE DOOR
TO . . . POETRY WRITING

POETRY WRITING

Some hints

Make a rough copy so that you can alter it where necessary.

If you are writing descriptive poetry, it may be useful to make a list of suitable words and phrases before you begin.

Samuel Taylor Coleridge stated that poetry is 'the best words in the best order'. Try to choose the best words and phrases you know – for example, it may be better to write 'a wild winter wind' rather than 'a rough, cold wind', even though both phrases mean the same thing.

Many words convey meaning through their sounds – for example, clip-clop, shimmering, silken. Listen to the sounds made by words and try to select words which will add colour to your 'word-picture'.

Poetry does not need to rhyme (refer to the section on free verse page 125) but if you wish to write in rhyme be careful not to sacrifice meaning simply to make words rhyme at the ends of lines. For example:

Noah, in his brand new ark
Sailed beside the green, green park.

This is obvious nonsense! Can you think of a more suitable second line?

If you are using a *particular* verse form, you must examine the rules and keep to them. (Refer to the sections on haiku, limericks and couplets.)

Remember that 'there is beauty in simplicity'; keep your writing simple and keep to the subject.

Limericks

1   There was an old man of Blackheath,
2   Who sat on his set of false teeth,
3   Said he, with a start,
4   'Oh Lord, bless my heart!
5   I've bitten myself underneath!'

NOTE

A limerick has five lines.

It has a particular rhyming scheme – lines 1, 2 and 5 rhyme and lines 3 and 4 rhyme. The rhyming scheme is a a b b a.

A limerick is also written to a particular rhythm. Lines 1, 2 and 5 have the same rhythm and lines 3 and 4 have a different, shorter rhythm. Re-read the example, concentrating on absorbing the 'feel' of the rhythm.

A limerick is always humorous.

Try writing your own limerick. Here are some suggestions:

> There once was a strange kangaroo

> A lady with hair full of lice

> A crone of extraordinary age

Couplets

1 Here lie the bones
2 of old Mr Jones

1 Swans sing before they die – 'twere no bad thing
2 Should certain persons die before they sing.

Coleridge

NOTE

A couplet has two lines.

The lines have the same number of beats – rhythm.

The words at the line-ends must rhyme with each other.

Poems may be composed of a series of couplets. Read 'Springboks' page 92 and the extract from 'Macbeth' page 109.

Haiku

1 Alone I cling to   (5)
2 The freezing mountain and see   (7)
3 White cloud – below me.   (5)

> Ian Serraillier

NOTE

Haiku originated in Japan. It is a very compact way of expressing an idea – usually about nature.

There are only *seventeen* syllables arranged in *three* lines. Five syllables in the first line, seven in the second and five in the third.

Free verse

Listen . . .
With a faint dry sound
Like steps of passing ghosts
The leaves, frost-crisped, break from the trees
And fall.

from 'November Night' Adelaide Crapsey

NOTE

Free verse means writing without any particular rhyme or rhythm.

The lines are arranged in a pattern to aid the meaning. It will help you if you imagine how the words and phrases would be spoken.

Read the above example. Why is 'Listen . . .' written as it is?

The poet has made excellent use of language. Say 'steps of passing ghosts' and listen to the soft sounds of the words. Now say 'frost-crisped' and notice the hard, brittle sound. When writing poetry, try to convey meaning through sounds made by the words you select.

Read 'The Door' by Miroslav Holub and 'The Beach' by Leonard Clark. Both are fine examples of free verse.

Rhyming verse

There are many different ways of arranging poetry so that it rhymes.

In the poems 'Smells' page 58 and 'Rain' page 19 each of the lines of each verse have the same end rhymes. It is very difficult to write this type of poetry.

The rhyme scheme is:

The lights are all on, though it's just past midday,   a
There are no more indoor games we can play,   a
No one can think of anything to say,   a
It rained all yesterday, it's raining today,   a
It's grey outside, inside it's grey.   a

In the poem 'A dragonfly' the second and fourth lines rhyme. This system is fairly simple to use.

The rhyme scheme is:

When the heat of the summer   a
Made drowsy the land,   b
A dragonfly came   c
And sat on my hand.   b

In the poem 'The Reformed Pirate' the lines rhyme in pairs or couplets.

The rhyme scheme is:

His proper name was Peter Sweet: a
But he was known as Keel-haul Pete   a
From Turtle Cay to Port-of-Spain   b
And all along the Spanish Main,   b
And up and down those spicy seas   c
Which lave the bosky Caribbees.   c

You will find that there are many other ways of arranging rhyme patterns.

INDEX OF TITLES

INDEX OF AUTHORS

INDEX OF FIRST LINES

Until I saw the sea 7

Voices moving about in the quiet house 26

We are going to see the rabbit 76
We are the bulldozers, bulldozers, bulldozers 119
What are they, these gliders in the blue, cold air 115
When I am an old woman I shall wear purple 54

When John was ten they gave the boy 83
When the heat of the summer 78
Whether the weather be fine 16
Who's that stopping at my door 108
Why is it that the poets tell 58
Witch rides off 108

Yellow sun yellow 93

ACKNOWLEDGEMENTS

Grateful acknowledgement is made to the following sources for permission to reproduce poems in this anthology, the titles of which are listed in the Index of Authors on pages 128 to 129.

A. R. Ammons, W. W. Norton & Co. Ltd; J. Redwood Anderson, Sidgwick & Jackson Ltd; Michael Baldwin, the author; R. N. Bartlett, the author; Guy Boas, Batsford Ltd and *Punch*; D. J. Brindley, Hodder & Stoughton Ltd; James Nimmo Britton, the author; Alan Brownjohn, Secker & Warburg Ltd; Roy Campbell, Curtis Brown; Hugh Chesterman, Basil Blackwell Ltd; Leonard Clark, Dobson Books Ltd; Adelaide Crapsey, Holmes McDougall Ltd; T. W. H. Crosland, Secker & Warburg Ltd; Roy Daniells, Oxford University Press, Toronto; Roald Dahl, Jonathan Cape Ltd; Richard Digance, Michael Joseph Ltd; Eleanor Farjeon, David Higham Associates Ltd; Rachel Field, Macmillan Publishing Co. Inc.; Flanders & Swann, Lister Welch Ltd; Melvin Walker la Follette, *The New Yorker*; Robert Frost, Jonathan Cape Ltd; Carmen Bernos de Gasztold, Macmillan Co., New York; Barrie Grayson, Ginn & Company Ltd; J. W. Hackett, Japan Publications Inc., Tokyo; Gregory Harrison, Bell & Hyman Ltd; A. P. Herbert, A. P. Watt Ltd and Lady Herbert; Phoebe Hesketh, the author and Chatto & Windus Ltd; Miroslav Holub, Penguin Books Ltd; Patricia Hubbell, Atheneum Publishers Ltd; Randall Jarrell, Faber & Faber Ltd; Pauline Johnson, the author; James Weldon Johnson, George Allen & Unwin Ltd; Jenny Josephs, John Johnson; James Joyce, The Executors of the Estate of James Joyce and Jonathan Cape Ltd; Jean Kenward, the author; James Kirkup, Curtis Brown; Maxine Kumin, Hodder & Stoughton Ltd; D. H. Lawrence, Laurence Pollinger Ltd and the Estate of Mrs Frieda Lawrence Ravagli; Will Lawson, Angus and Robertson (UK) Ltd; Brian Lee, Penguin Books Ltd; Walter de la Mare, the Literary Trustees and The Society of Authors; Don Marquis, Doubleday & Company Inc.; Eve Merriam, Penguin Books Ltd and International Creative Management, New York; Spike Milligan, Michael Joseph Ltd and Dobson Books Ltd; Lilian Moore, the author and Atheneum Publishers Ltd; Christopher Morley, Methuen & Co.; Carole Paine, *Punch*; E. J. Pratt, University of Toronto Press; Elizabeth du Preez, the author; Jack Prelutsky, Greenwillow Books; Knud Rasmussen, World Publishing Co. Ltd; James Reeves, William Heinemann Ltd; T. G. Roberts, McGraw-Hill Ryerson Ltd, Toronto; W. W. E. Ross, Longman Canada Ltd, Toronto; Carl Sandburg, Harcourt Brace Jovanovich Inc.; Siegfried Sassoon, G. T. Sassoon; Ian Serraillier, the author; Rodney Sivyour, Longman Group Ltd; Ruth Skilling, the author; William Stafford, Harper & Row Publishers Inc., New York; Margaret Stanley-Wrench, Donald D. Derrick; Bruce Stronach, Maskew Miller; James Stephens, Mrs Iris Wise and The Society of Authors; R. S. Thomas, Granada Publishing Ltd; John Walsh, Mrs Mary Walsh; John Welsh, William Heinemann Ltd; Kit Wright, Fontana Paperbacks; Peter Young, Oliver & Boyd.

The publishers and compilers regret that they have been unable to trace the copyright owners of poems by the following authors and will be pleased to rectify any such omission in future editions:

Berta Lawrence, G. K. Menzies, Francis Carey Slater, N. D. H. Spicer.

Thanks are also due to the following copyright holders for permission to reproduce illustrations:

Page 1, Camera Press; 15, Howard Jay: 18, 19, 40, 66/67, 73, 89, 112, *The Sunday Chronicle*, Bulawayo; 53, *Yours*, newspaper; 57, *The Times Educational Supplement*; 104, Megan Lewis. The remainder of the illustrations are by Margaret Peek.